Praise for *The Human Side*

"My good friend John Passante has spent his career assisting companies to develop and nurture cultures which drive positive results and with a keen eye and appreciation for the wonderful qualities of human nature. His wisdom will inspire leaders to lead with courage."

—KATHLEEN SCHMATZ, PRESIDENT AND CEO,
AUTOMOTIVE AFTERMARKET INDUSTRY ASSOCIATION

"One of the biggest challenges most organizations face today is keeping people focused on the 'right things.' No matter how big or small the operation, staying on target is the key to achieving results and steering everyone in the right direction. In this outstanding book, John Passante shares his wit and wisdom to help all of us remember what's important in leadership: the human touch."

—MIKE FIORITO, VICE PRESIDENT, KYB AMERICA

"I have known John for many years. I always admired his unique way of dealing with people issues that seemed to be a part of our lives in the arena that we know as the automotive aftermarket. With his broad experience within this large marketplace, he always seemed to be the person we turned to when there was a people problem. He didn't get the title of doctor by accident … he earned it."

—JACK CREAMER, PRESIDENT OF DISTRIBUTION MARKETING SERVICES AND FORMER
PRESIDENT OF THE AUTOMOTIVE WAREHOUSE DISTRIBUTORS ASSOCIATION (AWDA)

"John Passante is a visionary individual who never forgets the importance of the critical human factor of leadership. He reminds us that in all things, people are people—no matter the industry, the economy or the century. I've had the honor of knowing John for 10 years, and am continually impressed and moved by his ability to connect with people and genuinely inspire them to greatness."

—LÚCIA VEIGA MORETTI, PRESIDENT, DELPHI PRODUCT & SERVICE SOLUTIONS

"John Passante's career has included stints in sales, operations and human resource management with some of the biggest and best automotive parts companies in the business. Through the years, I've consulted with him on numerous projects and I've always found him to be thoughtful and focused on how to get the best out of our human capital. John has always been a 'people' person and his care for others comes through in everything he does. His book is no exception."

—DAVID PEACE, PRESIDENT, WELLS VEHICLE ELECTRONICS

"Over the course of your career, you meet people who have a profound impact on your development. In my case, John Passante is someone who has helped me in many ways. His dynamic personality, his teaching methods and his core philosophy are inspiring. His insights into the human side of business have helped me and many others become better managers. If the challenge in life is to bring out the best in those around us, John shows us how to do that. He has no equal … he is the best!"

—MORT SCHWARTZ, FOUNDING PARTNER, SCHWARTZ ADVISORS

"John Passante has a unique understanding of the human impact on a company's success and the fulfillment of the spirit of the individual. His passion for effective leadership and mentoring of people who desire to make meaningful contributions and receive recognition is unparalleled. John has provided extensive leadership in the automotive industry for developing proper management techniques and improving motivation of personnel, leading to higher results and job satisfaction. His dedication to continuous improvement in both process and personnel provides a recipe for success in today's competitive environment."

—LARRY PAVEY, PRESIDENT, FEDERATED AUTO PARTS

the Human Side

High-Touch Leadership in a High-Tech World

By John A. Passante
Edited by Gary McCoy

Published by
The Organizational Development Group
Fairway Communications

ISBN: 978-0-615-84456-5

Published by The Organizational Development Group
Fairway Communications

Printed in the United States of America

My Inspiration

My Irish angel and wife, Margaret, for always believing in me. You have been my rock and true inspiration. You are my beacon of true faith and love.

Julie and Amy, my remarkable daughters, who have taught me many things about life and love. You are women of conviction and compassion.

Tom, Brian, Boone, Callahan, Tate, Cecelia, Johnny, Sophia and Abigail, you are treasured gifts and a blessing.

My mother, who always faced adversity with class and dignity.

Eileen, Tony, Kathy, Jimmy and Heather, for your love and support.

Contents

The Human Side: Dedicated to the Memory of Larry W. McCurdy
By Joseph Onorato

This book is dedicated to Larry W. McCurdy, a highly respected leader within the automotive aftermarket for many years who passed away in 2010 at the age of 75.

Larry held executive positions with several of the industry's best known companies. In his last assignment, he was chairman of the board of Affinia Group Inc. He had served in that role since the company's inception in 2004.

I had the privilege of working with and knowing Larry personally. He invented the term "Zero Dark Thirty," because he was always in the office before sunrise to get everything done he needed to accomplish.

Larry had the charisma to inspire an entire organization and to always establish high standards for himself and everyone around him. Larry was a remarkable leader who during times of extreme pressure remained focused on the goal at hand and consistently supported his management team. He was a lighthouse for the aftermarket, a beacon that shined a light for doing the right thing in an industry that often struggled to find direction.

He lived a life committed to a high moral code and nurtured a culture of true teamwork and accountability. Communications were open and candid, but always professional.

Larry taught us to think and was always encouraging. Here's how Terry R. McCormack, president and CEO of Affinia Group, remembers Larry: "He was a true leader in every sense of the word. He was always generous with his knowledge, his time and his trusted relationships within the industry. Larry served as a wise and patient mentor to our management team and was very instrumental in helping us formulate our global strategies. We greatly miss his valued counsel and his warm friendship."

Larry facilitated change and carefully guided the actions required. Larry was truly a man of character and faith who sought out the best in others. He was a steward who looked out for all he touched by his leadership. He was a fair, committed, hard-working, focused and customer friendly businessman who earned the respect of an entire industry.

He was a results-driven chief executive who was man enough to show his human side! Those of us who had the honor of working with Larry are better for the life-changing and impactful experiences he shared with us.

Larry was missed greatly the day he left us and the world will forever be a lesser place without him. Our industry lost a pillar and all of us lost a friend. Everyone deserves a Larry McCurdy in their life.

Foreword

By Rollie Massimino

During my career I've coached hundreds of young men in basketball and more importantly in the game of life. One thing I've always emphasized is the vital role of character.

I've enjoyed the opportunity to get to know John Passante. He is a kindred spirit who understands that character is indispensable, whether you are playing basketball or running a company. He believes that leadership, responsibility and communications are vital. John believes in the power of the human spirit!

In this outstanding book on leadership, John has tapped into his background in the automotive aftermarket to help readers understand that the human side of the leadership equation is often a vital and missing piece. Though technology has changed and has helped improve our lives, John reminds us that the way you treat people hasn't changed. You must treat everyone fairly, and do so with all your heart and soul.

I was recently listening to a radio program where a group of CEOs were being interviewed on how to make their workforces better. They mentioned things like more productivity and accountability. At the end of their discussion, they came to the conclusion that it wasn't days off, higher salaries or benefits that made the difference. It was caring and sharing that employees wanted most from their leaders.

Average leaders remain aloof and distant, but great leaders take time to engage with the people under their charge. The best leaders understand it's not a weakness to get personal, to display empathy, kindness and compassion. John Passante reminds us that it's actually the ultimate strength.

I highly recommend that you take time to read and digest this book. I guarantee it will help make you a better leader.

Acknowledgments

It is important for me to express my gratitude and appreciation for my extraordinary editor, Gary McCoy. He was always supportive and helpful in the process of writing this book. His Iowa value system and care for others always showed through.

Gary is a committed professional with an appreciation for all that is human. He is a skilled journalist and a focused executive who is always mindful of the importance of bringing out the best in others.

I am thankful to Terry McCormack, president and CEO of Affinia, for his belief in my message and me.

Both Terry and I have had the blessing of working for and with Larry W. McCurdy, a man of true vision, drive, dedication, responsibility, integrity and enthusiasm. He was a man of goodness and faith. He set higher standards for himself than he did for others. He had faith in himself and others and committed his life to making better all that he influenced in business. His was a heroic journey that he lived with crystal clear focus, sound judgment and a mindfulness of his impact on others. He always valued the opinions of others, sought to bring out the best in people, had a laser view of the human spirit and encouraged us all to reach our human potential.

Introduction

One cannot write a book about the human touch and human experience without engaging in a great deal of self-reflection and introspection.

Many people influenced the stories that flow through each chapter. They all influenced me, touched me with their daily practice of seeking to make me better as a man and as a leader. The journey of leadership is to embrace one's gifts, to value each relationship and to always marvel in the glory of the need we all have for acceptance in this life.

I continue to be unbridled in my belief and passion for the capabilities of each of us to conquer issues and to create a better and more enlightened work environment through a commitment to and keen awareness of the true power of the human touch.

Our collective mission is to act as role models, to serve as park rangers (in the park called life) guiding the people we encounter each day with compassion, and to become stewards for each other. Let us take the time from this hectic business world to become leaders grounded in the joys of meaningful relationships, integrity, openness, trust, mutual support, respect and kindness. Hopefully we will never lose sight of the true possibilities of an organization and society where each day we awaken with the mission and faith to touch others in order to make their day better and more rewarding.

"If you would not be forgotten as soon as you are dead and rotten, either write things worth reading or do things worth the writing," said Benjamin Franklin, one of our wise founding fathers.

I have been working since I was 10 years old. I started by having two paper routes in Pekin, Illinois, then became a caddy, set pins in a bowling alley, became a mechanic on the automatic pinsetters, worked at a service station and spent almost four years in the United States Air Force. I also painted houses, was a welder in a Chevrolet transmission plant and worked as an accountant. Ultimately, I moved into the human resources profession and continue to be heavily involved in organizational development, general management and sales and marketing. I also became an adjunct college professor teaching at the MBA level.

I owe a debt of gratitude to the people who have worked with me and taught me about business relationships, empathy, leadership and the magic of the human condition. I appreciate my clients, students and friends in whom I have stoked the fire of the human touch.

My writings are, to some degree, a letter about the journey and experiences I have had over the years. I am excited to share these with family, friends, students and clients.

I am a passionate humanist who believes in the power of the human spirit, which is released in all of us by *The Human Touch*.

The truth remains in the final analysis—people are the answer!

John A. Passante, July 2013

Chapter 1

What is the Human Side of Leadership?

As one who has spent most of my career in the automotive aftermarket, I have witnessed many remarkable changes over the past 35–plus years. When I began my career, most of the companies in the aftermarket were family-owned. These were iconic firms like Monroe Auto Equipment Company, Champion Spark Plugs, MOOG Automotive and Fel-Pro, along with hundreds of warehouse distributors and jobber stores throughout the United States and Canada.

As a result, the company cultures were indeed paternalistic—family—in the truest sense. Employees felt a high degree of belonging. Communications were open and came from the heart, as well as the head. If a family member was sick and hospitalized, flowers arrived from the CEO. Whatever the size of the organization, leaders displayed sincere empathy and built rapport.

All of us who started our careers in the '70s believed we would work for the same company for 30 or 40 years, then happily retire. There was a sense of loyalty, pride and security. The employer and the employee had a verbal contract called: "We are in this together!"

The vision of the early days of the automotive aftermarket was that the customer was king—and every employee was a member of the sales team.

The Human Side drove decisions. It was built by organizations who placed human beings (employees) at the center of their value proposition and concerns. These shared common goals were rooted in the magic of mutually beneficial relationships, both internal as well as external.

The management style of the day was humanistic. The beacon of light we followed was lifetime employment (unless you really did something quite tragic). The industry was growing, year over year. Most employees knew the president and CEO, as well as the executive staff, on a first name basis.

The leaders of the day did an excellent job balancing human behavior and organizational performance, both informal and formal. Positive emotions were encouraged, as were negative emotions. The test was: Do these emotions address what is best for the organization? Emotions drive behavior, exert strong influence on employees' decisions and impact commitment levels. Leaders clearly understood that if the informal organization is not working for you, it is working against you. Additionally, leaders were keenly aware that they did not have all the answers. So spending time with all levels of employees to seek out their ideas, concerns and creativity was a good use of time.

Let me be clear, I am not saying that everything was perfect in the early days of the aftermarket and the business world in general. That was certainly not the case. I am just attempting to capture the mood of the day.

The landscape of today's business world has clearly changed. Both manufacturers and distributors are, for the most part, no longer family-owned. The watchwords of the day are consolidation, mergers, and acquisitions. The global economy continues to pressure companies to do more with less.

As a pragmatic businessman, I understand this. My contention is that more than ever we need to be sensitive to the importance of: *The Human Side of the Business Enterprise*. Some call this the *soft side* of the business.

The business model of today requires scalability—the potential of a business to continue to function effectively as its size increases. In the pursuit of scalability, companies typically focus on financial, technological or physical resources. These resources are more readily available today than human talent. Is there a scarcity of talent in your organization? Are you concerned about your succession planning progress? Leaders aware of the human side believe they should

> Leaders aware of the human side believe they should commit to developing their people through coaching and training.

commit to developing their people through coaching and training. Scalability in essence means that CEOs must become leaders of tomorrow's leaders.

We live in a high-tech world, with more technology on its way. Each day more than a billion people sign on to the Internet for business, communication and to research everything, such as political issues, the economy, high school term papers and complex medical information. The data is instant and easily available. Of course, all this is positive, if the information and resources are utilized properly without overshadowing the human side of the enterprise.

For example, I am concerned when I hear that long-service employees with 20 or 30 years of experience are told their job has been eliminated via email. Or when text messages replace a well-deserved *pat on the back!*

As a leader, when was the last time you had a meaningful conversation with an employee regarding his or her future with the company, or showed true interest in a project that an employee was working on?

More than ever before, the business world needs hands-on leadership with vision and a passion for the human side to go with modern technology. Whatever industry you work in, it is time to engage all your employees to help get the message out that your sector of the economy offers challenging career opportunities along with a strong human side.

It appears that the business environment will become more complex in the coming years. Success will require more creativity on the part of the organizations and their human side (employees) and will entail changing our work cultures. It will involve unlearning and selectively forgetting past success formulas so that we can create new value propositions, products and relationships with employees, customers and external partners. The human side drives bottom-up participation and flexible thinking inspired by a human approach to leadership.

You will find that true leadership becomes a richer and deeper experience when leaders feel they are part of a cause that is greater than themselves. It's called the human side!

In the upcoming chapters of this book, you will be exposed to the legacy of leadership, the importance of mentoring, soul searching, the importance of enthusiasm, the personal side of business, the impact of attitude, the power of storytelling, time management, customer passion, sales management and more!

As you travel the business highway ahead, be sure to utilize your GPS (Good People Skills). Balance your daily tasks with the human side of your business. Do not view your employees as a head count number on a human resource

Tales from the front lines

One Leader Who Turned to the Human Side

A few years ago I coached an extremely driven, bottom line focused president and CEO. Frankly, he viewed employees as a cost. We spent many hours discussing the purpose and impact of leadership. I shared my view that most employees have a keen passion and desire to contribute each day. He was skeptical but listened intensely. (He was in fact intense most of the time).

The company was going through some difficult business challenges, i.e. aggressive competition, price wars, etc. Adding to the stress, the CEO's mother was experiencing serious health issues which kept him out of the office for a week. His mother ended up passing away while he was with her. When he returned, his senior staff presented him with a strategic, and well-thought-out business plan which addressed the company's challenges. The plan consisted of financial charts, marketing programs, new pricing and company reorganization.

I was invited to the presentation by the senior staff, so I had the chance to observe the CEO as each executive presented a portion of the business plan. I keenly watched his verbal reaction to the information, as well as his facial expression.

During my coaching sessions with him, I had reviewed the power of emotional intelligence to the success of an organization. Emotional intelligence is the ability to identify, assess, and control the emotions of report or as a cost center on your financial report. View employees as a jewel that you can polish and make shine.

Wayne Dyer, an internationally renowned author and speaker in the field of self-development, said, "When you change the way you look at things, the things you look at change."

Enjoy the ride on the human side.

oneself, of others, and of groups. For leaders, emotional intelligence is a way to appropriately channel their personal passions and to be authentic. Emotional intelligence is only part of the equation, it must be added with the talents, optimism, tenacity and determination of the organization's employees. Clearly, the CEO was both impressed and emotional during the business planning meeting.

I was asked to speak at the conclusion of this key meeting. I reminded the CEO that his staff had risen to the occasion during his absence. They had worked more than 75 hours that week in order to address these business challenges and support him on a personal and professional basis.

When I ended my remarks, the CEO looked at me with a tear in his eye and said, "John, I get it!" The light went on!

That night over a drink, this leader acknowledged that people skills were important and he needed to continue to have faith in his team. He rightly stated, "There is nothing soft about believing in others."

What was the lesson this leader learned? The more opportunities he gives his employees to grow and add value, the more the company will benefit and so will the employees.

The lesson this leader learned is to view people through the lens of *the glance of mercy*, which means to view other human beings with acceptance and understanding.

The Human Side

Chapter 2

The Impact and Purpose of Leadership

Business professionals in today's competitive, fast-paced and intense economy often have little time to reflect on the importance and impact of leaders. As you read this chapter, I encourage you to take a moment from your hectic schedule and think of the leaders that have influenced you the most.

Hopefully, it doesn't take long to come up with the names of those *special* people who impacted you and the characteristics of their leadership style.

The significance of leadership is this: it sets the tone at the top, it establishes the culture in an organization and people mirror the example they see. In other words, the behavior, the style, the value systems, the methods, the communications and the trust factor that the leader either engenders or doesn't engender has an impact on performance, motivation and self-esteem.

When I lead seminars across the country, I say, "The most important thing to evaluate in a person's life is how he or she impacts another human being."

> Leadership is all about making an impact on those around you.

That's what leadership is all about: making an impact on those around you. It involves granting people the opportunity to use their God-given talents.

So what are the characteristics of strong and effective leaders who make an impact? I would like to share some of the insights I've gleaned about leadership in my 35-plus years as a human resources and organizational development executive for large- and medium-sized global corporations.

Let's first look at some general characteristics of leaders. My experience and research clearly indicate that true leaders display passion. They have a passion for life, being successful, making a difference and leading positive change in their enterprise.

This style of authentic leadership builds trust, and trust is the basis of all relationships. The mantra of leadership is to earn the right to lead each day. Trust must be enhanced and polished every day.

> The mantra of leadership is to earn the right to lead each day.

As an organization experiences change, it is incumbent for the leader to communicate with clarity, consistency and commitment.

Another important characteristic is humility. It is quite interesting to me that the higher you move in an organization, the fewer things employees tell you. Why? Because we all know that many times the messenger does indeed get shot. As a leader it is paramount to be able to humbly accept the truth—the good, the bad and the ugly.

Humility extends to the way leaders handle employees. It is important to remember to attack issues and not people. When leaders attack people, it shuts down the truth, creativity and problem-solving. There is no question that leaders must have healthy egos, but they cannot satisfy their egos at the expense of others.

All of us respect and admire leaders with vision, conviction and sincere confidence. The leaders that are heroes to you and me need to be keenly aware of the impact they have on the company and its associates.

Without question, leaders' attitudes make the weather in the companies they lead. By this I mean that if the organizational leader is in a stormy mood, everyone knows it. Negative moods by the leader can drain productivity, foster negative attitudes and may impact customer service for both internal and external customers.

There are many more characteristics of good leaders, but these are some of the most important. Let me conclude with four important roles that leaders can play: conductor, connector, challenger and caregiver.

Conductor—A leader is like a symphony orchestra's conductor who strives to maintain melodious performance while responding to issues both internal and external. Leaders have formal roles in an organization. They have authority and status. They wear numerous hats—spokesperson for the vision of the firm, decision maker, resource allocator, handler, mentor and pacesetter. Effective leadership builds positive relationships throughout the company.

Connector—Leaders play important roles: developing supportive relationships, carrying on negotiations, motivating subordinates, resolving conflicts, establishing key information networks, disseminating information, making decisions in conditions that constantly change

> All of us respect and admire leaders with vision, conviction and sincere confidence.

and then allocating the proper resources in order to correct or resolve a problem and or issue. Without question, leadership is not for the faint of heart. A connected leader must have the ability to prepare the organization for constant change and help employees cope as they work in a world of global competition, real-time technology and increased pressure to do more with less.

Challenger—Leaders who have made a difference in our lives are those who put an emphasis on creating challenging opportunities for their employees. They pushed responsibility our way, which made our jobs more exciting and rewarding. These high impact leaders recognized our contributions and rewarded us with praise and, in many cases, more responsibilities.

Caregiver—We live in a high-tech, low-touch world. Employees seek leadership that understands the importance of the human touch. The power and potential of employees is unlimited; when human beings put their mind and spirit into something, that's when magic occurs. Employees have a strong desire to contribute and achieve, and they hunger to be recognized. The question behind the question: When is the last time you complimented an associate? When is the last time you showed your human side? Today is the day to empathize, listen with care or send a positive email to someone.

Take a moment to contemplate your leadership style.

- How do you measure up?
- Do you foster and solicit open feedback from your team?
- Are you making a positive impact on your organization?
- Are you setting a good tone at the top?

Tales from the front lines

The Impact of Caring

I will never forget Christmas Eve 1992. Late in the afternoon my phone rang at home. It was the human resources manager from our plant in Maryville, Mo. He said, "John, I have some very bad news to share with you, and I feel terrible spoiling your Christmas Eve." My response was, "Okay, Dave, please let me have it."

He said, "John, last night we had a storm and thick fog in Maryville. You could not see one foot in front of you. This morning the payroll manager went into the plant to work. When she opened the front door of the office, she smelled smoke. She went into the plant in order to determine if there was a problem. The door collapsed when she opened it, because the plant had burnt down during the night." To say I was in shock was an understatement.

I asked Dave if anyone was hurt, and thankfully he said, "No." The plant was down for the holiday, and of course my mind was racing. I told Dave I would call him back after I called Larry W. McCurdy, the president and CEO of MOOG. Trust me, no one wants to call his boss on Christmas Eve with this type of message.

I collected myself and called Larry. After informing him about what had happened, Larry said, "Let's have a conference call with the plant manager and the HR manager." We did. The decision was made that Larry and I would fly to Maryville on December 26 and meet with all the employees at the local community college.

One of my favorite sayings that I impart when I lead a workshop or seminar is this: "In the final analysis, people are the answer." In leadership, people are the critical difference.

On the flight to the plant, Larry asked me what we should do for the employees. I said we should continue to pay them and provide benefits for at least 60 days. Larry said he would need to ponder that for a while.

It was a cold, rainy day when we landed in Maryville. We went to the college that night to a huge gathering of 130 plant employees. The mood was one of concern and sadness.

A microphone was set up for Larry and me to talk to the group. Larry spoke first and told the employees that we would rebuild the plant, and do it quickly. There was a tremendous round of applause.

Then Larry said, "John A. Passante will talk to you about the continuation of pay and benefits." Once more there was an applause. When I stood up to speak, Larry whispered in my ear, "Give them four months of pay and benefits."

Larry made me look like the hero, but the truth is, he made the decision. On the plane ride back to St. Louis, Larry said, "John, leadership is always doing the right thing for employees."

As the late Paul Harvey would say, "Here's the rest of the story." We rented space at the community college and started manufacturing three months later. We rebuilt the Maryville plant in less than a year and *no one* lost their job. A decision was made on that Christmas Eve which impacted 130 families. As a result, it nurtured a special bond between our employees and the company.

Here's the message for leaders to remember: It is okay to show that you care.

The Human Side

Chapter 3

Meaningful Conversations in a High-Tech World

Without question, the Internet and Google have changed the world forever. We live in a world with access to as much information as we need or can seek on a particular subject. For the most part this is a good thing.

My concern is this: Has our business world lost the art of—and interest in—having a conversation with the customer? Are we relying too heavily on emails, text messages, blogs, etc.? We have content for customers, but how often do we have contact?

Relationships in every industry I've been associated with have been built and nourished on meaningful conversations. Few things are in fact more pleasurable than engaging in a good talk. Conversations with other people teach us how the world works. They force us to clarify our perspective, as well as recall our experiences.

The pressures in today's business environment can result in the lack of time to focus on this most basic human activity. Sad to say, non-goal-oriented conversations are a luxury in business today. We are all *time poor.*

I see people checking their smartphones in business meetings, over dinner, at sporting events, while pushing their child on a swing and yes, even during church services. This method of *conversing* makes a loud statement. Texting is often more important than listening and actually paying attention to the situation we are in. We choose not to stay in the moment.

Ask yourself this question: *Are healthy human conversations an endangered species?*

Face-to-face conversations are the foundation for understanding, problem solving, healthy debate, intimacy and knowledge. They are also a form of touch.

In my opinion, it is not only rude to look down at a handheld device rather than into the eyes of your conversation mate; it prevents the exchange of nonverbal cues that help generate rich and meaningful attachments. We *touch* people with our eyes.

A poem written by Spencer Michael Free clearly states the power of the human touch. Free graduated from the College of Physicians and Surgeons of the Johns Hopkins University in 1880, and practiced medicine and surgery for some 50 years thereafter. In addition to some 100 medical papers, he wrote many poems, including "The Human Touch," which has been widely quoted.

The Human Touch
'Tis the human touch
in this world that counts,
The touch of your hand and mine,
Which means far more
to the fainting heart
Than shelter and bread and wine.
For shelter is gone
when the night is o'er,
And bread lasts only a day.
But the touch of the hand
And the sound of the voice
Sing on in the soul always.

We cannot touch others over the Internet.

As Stanford sociologist Clifford Nass, author of "The Man Who Lied to His Laptop: What Machines Teach Us about Human Relationships," puts it, "Face-to-face social interaction is hard. If we don't go through a period where we're forced to master the hideous process of learning how to talk with other people, we never will."

Digital communication can breed confusion. As email communicators, we *hear* what we are writing based on our intentions. On the other hand, the recipient of our email may miss the nuance. We can all cite experiences where we sent a well-intended email and received the opposite intended reaction.

Ponder this: Would you rather receive an email telling you that your promotion was approved or would you rather be congratulated face-to-face? The written word does not always convey our true emotions that express joy, love, concern and compassion.

Quite honestly, we all seek the full attention of others. There is nothing like a person who is there just for you. Clearly, emails, text messages and social media allow us to stay in touch more than ever, but perhaps in a less thoughtful way.

It is a fact that email and social networking sites like Facebook encourage a quantity of relationships over quality. Today, people share intimate details through emails, and these powerful technology-driven communication tools are efficient and productive.

Let the word go forth. I am not against technology, emails, web blasts, texting, blogs, etc. As business professionals, let's find quality time for open discourse and active conversation. Leaders need to allow time for creative conversation to foster solutions and stoke the fire of passion that made the industry you are part of what it is today.

Anyone can use Google to find the answer to any question in seconds, but the real learning takes place in the ability to discern which information is factual and how to utilize the knowledge. This takes place in a face to face

> Leaders need to allow time for creative conversation to foster solutions.

exchange with another human being and the ability to impart wisdom not just information. This can only be done through the human touch.

I believe in the power of the human spirit and the power of conversations. Consider this:

- Conversations give us energy; they also generate energy and act as a catalyst for action.
- Conversations help us to relate to others (customers, employees, family, friends, etc.). They also help us to think and to develop new ideas and concepts.

- Conversations help us see the world from a different perspective.
- Conversations assist us in understanding the need for change.

Technology has indeed enhanced our ability to stay in touch, but conversations provide the true *human touch*. Content and human contact is a winning

Tales from the front lines

Technology Cannot Replace Compassion and Empathy

I will never forget the phone call I received during a cold and dreary New England day in the winter of 2008. I was working late on a Friday afternoon in my home office when my phone rang. The caller identified himself and said, "John, I need someone to talk to. Do you have the time?"

I replied, "Not only do I have time to talk, but more importantly, I have time to listen!"

The caller was a business associate who had attended several of my seminars and someone I saw frequently at various industry meetings. By the tone of his voice, it was easy to detect that something bad had occurred. I asked how I could assist him.

He told me that upon graduation from college, he went to work for his current employer and had been with them for 27 years. He was a sales manager with a good professional reputation. He was speaking fast and said, "John, I have always made my sales numbers and been loyal to my employer."

He told me that the company to which he had given nearly three decades of his life had sent him an email telling him his position was being eliminated due to a reorganization. His employment was to be terminated, effective the following Monday.

His mood swung between anger, frustration, panic and disbelief.

When I pointed out that the economy in 2008 was quite difficult for all businesses, he yelled, "John, I know that!"

combination and the base for a great conversation. Let's all ensure that the art of a *good conversation* does not get lost in today's high tech world.

So if you would like to talk, I promise to listen!

Given the way in which he was treated, he planned to retaliate against his employer. He was the only employee with computer files on one of the company's top accounts, and he was going to delete them.

I gave him my professional view. First, I empathized, acknowledging his pain and appropriate anger. Then I told him this was not the time to act unprofessionally. I shared my father's advice that during times of adversity, "always take the high road." I told him adversity does not build character, it reveals it.

He seemed to calm down a little. I recommended that he start to think about the future. "Look through the windshield and not the rearview mirror."

I offered to help him put together a first-class resume and hone his interviewing skills. At this point he laughed and said, "Okay John, I feel a little better. Thanks for being a good listener."

Then I asked the magic question: "Are you going to delete those files?" He laughed again and said, "John, of course not. I am taking the high road."

I enjoyed working with him on his search. Four months later, he accepted a key position as director of sales with a global organization. He's still there today performing at the highest level.

I believe technology is an efficient and timeless way to communicate. However, when you influence an employee's life in a significant way, through a promotion, transfer, or termination, it should be done in person with facts, compassion and the human touch.

The Human Side

Chapter 4

Silence is Not Feedback

There are certain events, experiences, meetings or requirements in life that we all dread. To name a few: going to your dentist for a root canal, attending a corporate budget review meeting, paying taxes, renewing your driver's license and, perhaps the most feared of all, the annual employee performance appraisal meeting.

At most companies, reviewing and evaluating employees is a requirement and many times they take place just prior to the year-end holiday season. So why spoil an employee's holiday by giving a poor appraisal?

Today's business environment is driven by strategic objectives, as well as metrics, which are monitored and reported on a quarterly basis. Sales/revenue performance, budget variances, market share growth, ROI, expense control, profit, etc. are all tracked diligently.

Many times when it comes to closely analyzing the job performance of employees, things become a little murky. This is a business discipline that I have been professionally involved in and studied for many years.

Most employees want to truthfully know how they measure up in the eyes of their boss. It is a human trait to desire feedback with regard to any endeavor that we feel is important and life changing.

I must emphatically state that silence is not feedback.

In some cases, leaders feel that if an employee reaches or exceeds their objectives and meets deadlines, it is not necessary to spend (waste) time discussing job performance or career goals. This of course can create an interesting situation. Since the employees receive little or no feedback, they could assume one of several options:

1. All is well.
2. My leader does not care.
3. I am being taken for granted.
4. There is a problem with my supervisor.

Think of any relationship where you received little or no feedback. How did it impact your communication and trust level?

The key to any worthwhile, productive and positive employee performance appraisal process is to establish personal business objectives that can be measured. I like to use a handy acronym—S.M.A.R.T.

S Specific

M Measurable

A Attainable

R Reach (stretch goals to reach their potential)

T Time-bound (trackable goals)

Goals should be mutually developed with the employee so there is buy-in. After all, we all need challenges and targets in order to feel alive and excited about the day. The goal setting process provides a solid foundation on which to begin evaluating employee performance. Either the goals were accomplished or not, and you can discuss with the employee why and how.

> A leader's expectations of employees and their expectations of themselves are key factors in how they perform.

The subjective aspect of evaluating employee performance centers on human behavior, which can be observed and measured Ask these questions to help formulate your evaluation:

- How does the employees act and behave in order to reach their goals?
- Do they run over other departments?

- Are they sensitive to building relationships with other members of the organization?
- Are they team players?

A leader's expectations of employees and their expectations of themselves are key factors in how they perform. Known as the Pygmalion Effect, the power of expectations cannot be overestimated. What you expect is what you get.

The Pygmalion Effect:
- Leaders have expectations of the employees that report to them.
- Leaders communicate their expectations consciously or unconsciously.
- Employees pick up on, or consciously or unconsciously read, these expectations.
- Employees perform in ways that are consistent with the expectations they have picked up on.
- The way leaders treat their subordinates is subtly influenced by what they expect of them.

How many employees in your organization clearly understand what is expected of them?

High expectations equal a higher level of performance. A low level of expectations equals a lower level of performance.

Feedback does matter. The only way employees improve is when their leader provides candid, supportive and timely performance feedback. In today's business environment, leaders have to evaluate what has changed, what should stay the same and what no longer works.

> Feedback plays a key role to help focus the employee and the organization.

Feedback plays a key role to help focus the employee and the organization.

If a leader has ideas and information that will help improve employee performance, it is a sin not to share it.

The keys to effective and meaningful employee performance reviews are:
- Mutually established employee performance goals which support the corporate objectives and mission statement.

- Specific goals that are measurable.
- Clearly articulated expectations and appropriate behaviors that employees understand and buy into.
- Regular meetings (at least once a quarter) with employees to track performance, offer support or change goals due to business conditions.
- Schedule employee reviews annually.

Tales from the front lines

Alignment is Key

As a veteran human resources executive and CEO, I have always been keen on clear company goals, objectives, open communication and alignment.

A shared understanding of goals, competencies and expectations is critical for corporate success. It fosters a corporate culture of continuous improvements and sets the stage for professional development. Performance feedback assists employees in improving, thus providing them support in achieving their goals.

During my nine years at MOOG Automotive, we generated a performance review system that was quite creative. The president and I met in large groups with all our employees. We communicated the overall company strategy for the upcoming year and handed out hard copies of the corporate goals for the new year. Each executive was asked to stand up at the meeting and articulate his or her goals for the year. Once again copies of the executives' goals were passed out to all of the employees.

The president and I then asked the assembled group of employees to take this information and develop their personal business goals with their direct supervisor. We committed to meet with all employees on a quarterly basis and give them an update on how well the company was achieving its objectives.

Paperwork does not equal feedback. Feedback is one human talking to another, on a subject that is important to both of them. Feedback will improve an employee's self-esteem and his or her willingness to succeed and contribute.

Remember silence is not feedback. Don't let your employees guess how they are doing. Believe in your people and they will return the favor.

Likewise, each executive, manager and supervisor would meet one-on-one with their direct reports on a quarterly basis to discuss progress being made toward their goals and to provide appropriate feedback. The focused process eliminated any surprises when year-end formal performance appraisals were conducted with each employee.

There is a strong correlation between a company's financial performance and an aligned goal setting process. When employees clearly understand their individual goals and how they relate to the company, they naturally become more engaged and involved. They understand how they contribute to the success of the company, and they work smarter.

At MOOG, tighter goal alignment and high goal visibility led to quicker execution of the company's strategy by allowing executive management to move more effectively across various objectives. By cascading and aligning the goal setting process, we created a corporate culture of shared responsibility that drove success. This approach increased goal visibility and boosted the idea of shared accountability.

And I must point out, we made our numbers and it was fun!

The Human Side

Chapter 5

Tell Me a Story

It has been said that words define us. In fact, certain statements or phrases conjure up strong emotions and memories. For example, remember when your daughter or son would say, "Tell me a story."

Most families have an uncle, aunt, grandparent, father or mother that will be asked, when a large group of family and friends gather around the Thanksgiving table, to recall a certain funny family event, story or memory. We all cherish these special times. I must admit that I am the storyteller in my family and each time I tell the story I add a little *Italian spice*.

According to Dr. Howard Gardner, a Harvard professor, "Storytelling is the single most powerful tool in a leader's toolkit." Every brand, every company and every experience has a story.

Clearly, data, statistics and facts tend to overwhelm us. Well-crafted and well-told stories assist in:

- Communicating the company vision
- Clarifying and perpetuating values
- Building awareness, agreement and a strong sense of community
- Shared successes and knowledge
- Engendering pride and a sense of achievement
- Shining light on how the company defines itself

In every industry, stories spread like wildfire driving excitement, engagement and motivation. They also create legacies that fuel organizations for generations.

Every organization is a living organism with a rich, emotional and very human history. Company stories tell us about founders, owners and influential leaders who gave birth to a dream and grew the business. They embody its rooted foundation and its wings of change and growth. Your company's stories need to be told. Stories stick. We all remember the story of Sam Walton and how he started Wal-Mart. Another businessman, Lee Iacocca, reduced his salary to one dollar while asking Chrysler employees to sacrifice.

In fact, stories *speak* to us. They appeal to our intellect and reason by providing evidence and information to bolster arguments, and they assist employees in making informed decisions emotionally. They bond organizations that share the same story and provide groups with a strong sense of belonging.

> Business storytelling makes a huge impact!

Stories, like your business model, sometimes need renewal. Business storytelling makes a huge impact!

Storytelling is uniquely a human endeavor. Stories are as old as humankind. Mythology from the ancient Greeks and Romans still permeates our culture today in the names of cars, planets and companies.

Stories boost employees' self-sufficiency. Listening to stories gives employees courage to overcome obstacles and strengthens belief in their own abilities to persevere and conquer fears. The stories that companies broadcast about themselves have a powerful impact on customers, shareholders and employees.

Stories have emotional appeal. We feel for other people through stories. We go through their joy, pain and journey with them. A well-crafted movie or book is a story that pulls you in emotionally. With the recent emergence of social media it is possible for one YouTube video to go *viral* and tell an amazing story that tugs at your heart strings.

Historically, we know that stories have played a key role in every industry to help transfer knowledge. To ensure our future, we must continue to spread the good news. Stories help align our mission, as well as support and document our company's rich history. Plus, they contain powerful emotions.

Stories are indeed part of the human spirit. They touch our personal core and provide a natural means for validating our personal and professional values.

Leadership involves creating a story: a vision that significantly affects the attitudes, thoughts, and behaviors of employees so they participate in positive change.

We respect and admire leaders in large part due to the personal stories they have shared with us. They pass on their passion and pure excitement for the future of their business and the industry they work in. In practice, storytelling can drive almost every aspect of the business environment from strategic planning to a complete transformation of the business enterprise.

> Company stories are uplifting and make employees a part of the story, which is truly an honor.

Perhaps it is time to focus less on PowerPoint presentations and more on telling the company story in a human and authentic way. Company stories are uplifting and make employees a part of the story, which is truly an honor.

Stories influence every facet of our lives. They are ubiquitous as the air we breathe, and as important. Harness their power. The next time a customer or an employee inquires about your business, tell them your story.

Before the printing press, stories had the power to move people and this still holds true today. Every company has a story and leaders should share the history with employees and customers.

You have a story, so be sure to pass it on. By the way, it is okay to exaggerate just a little.

Tales from the front lines

Angelo: The Story Behind the Interview

In late 1970, I worked as the vice president of organizational development for a company that wanted to hire a technical person to check their product for wearability, safety and longevity. A short time after I advertised for the job. I had many resumes to choose from and started the interview process.

The third gentleman I interviewed was named Angelo. An outgoing and effervescent man in his '60s, Angelo had immigrated to the United States from Italy where he had been a marble mason, electrician and painter. I was taken with his personality and zest for life, as was the hiring manager. In short, we offered him the job and Angelo accepted.

A week later I received a call from the director of engineering, concerned that Angelo had not shown up for his first day of employment. I called Angelo's home and was told by his wife, who spoke very little English that Angelo was in the hospital. I called the director of engineering back and recommended that we do nothing until we had more details. He agreed.

Three days later Angelo called me. He said, "Mr. Passante, I am out of the hospital and am ready to go to work next week." I replied, "Angelo, what happened?" He answered, "Mr. Passante, I had a double hernia, and I didn't think it was fair for the company insurance to pay for my operation. So I had my injury repaired at my own expense." What a refreshing attitude.

Of course, I was overwhelmed that this gentleman would do something like this. I told him to get a doctor's permission slip authorizing him to return to work. At once, I called the director of engineering and we agreed that a man of Angelo's character was worth waiting for.

Right on schedule two weeks later, Angelo reported for work. He was the oldest employee in the technical center but everyone loved him. He always had a smile on his face.

About a month later, the director of engineering and I were at a staff meeting. He said, "John, I have got to tell you what Angelo's been up to." I held my breath and waited. He replied, "Angelo arrives here about 6:15 a.m., makes the coffee and starts to work."

He continued, "As you are aware, we have a test track. At the center of the field Angelo has planted tomatoes and cucumbers." That summer he gave many employees fresh tomatoes and cucumbers.

Angelo did not have a formal education. He was self-taught and self-motivated. His zest for life was infectious, and he was not only respected by his coworkers, he was loved.

The point is, we all have a life story. The key is to listen.

The Human Side

Chapter **6**

Mentors Matter

It has been said that confession is good for the soul. So here goes. I entered the business world before mentors existed (at least formally or by definition). Of course, I would be less than honest if I did not state that I was fortunate enough to have senior executives who took an interest in me and nurtured my career, as well as guided me personally.

Let me tap into some movie references to support the idea of mentoring. First think of "Star Wars," with Yoda providing guidance to the young Luke Skywalker. "Train yourself to let go of everything you fear to lose."

Or think of the good witch Glinda in "The Wizard of Oz" providing guidance to Dorothy Gale. "You don't need to be helped any longer. You've always had the power to go back to Kansas."

> Mentoring is the glue that holds the organization together.

During challenging times, it is easy to pay little attention to mentoring, a key component of the *human side* of the business. However, all companies can benefit from implementing a mentoring program. Here's why:

- Mentoring is the glue that holds the organization together. It can increase employee retention and it clearly demonstrates that the company has an interest in its employees.
- It can assist the company in developing career paths that match the needs of both the employee and the company.

- It should be an integral part of the company's succession planning process.
- It's an investment in the company's human capital, promoting high potential employees as well as developing underperformers.
- It bridges competency gaps and encourages personal individual growth.

The first step is to identify your high performers—employees with strong potential who have the desire, drive and ability to grow within your corporation. The second step is to train executives, managers and supervisors to mentor, especially those who have a keen interest in assisting others in developing, utilizing their talents and pursuing their dreams.

The role of the mentor includes:

- Serving as a teacher and a motivator. The mentor is someone the employee admires and respects. In many cases, employees seek to model themselves and their career after that of their mentor.
- Functioning as a G.P.S. (Great Professional Skills) system. According to a Harvard Business Review article by Dorie Clark (March 2011), "Employees need to change their image by: Defining their destination. Where do they want to spend their energy?"
- Helping employees reinvent themselves.
- Leveraging employees' points of difference. What is their personal value proposition? What sets them apart?
- Showing new skills to those they mentor.
- Asking insightful questions: What do you stand for? What are your values? What do you believe in? What are your career goals? What are you willing to do to achieve them? What brings you joy? What do you desire from life? Who are your heroes? These are not easy questions. However, mentors require employees to look in the mirror and discover who they are and who they are not. And to address candidly and professionally what the employee wants to do about these discoveries.

Mentoring is based on mutual trust, respect, objective goal setting and candid, supportive feedback and unlocks employees' talents and desires. Mentors function as a source of positive energy. They should guide and strive to provide employees with inspiration, motivation and vitality.

How do you select mentors?

- Recruit mentors who have vision, conviction, character and courage. They see things and opportunities that others do not.

> Mentors function as a source of positive energy.

- Both the mentor and the mentee must have mental and emotional fortitude. Professional and personal growth require courage. The key is to be open and authentic with each other.

If you were an employee, why would you seek a mentor?

- To guide you toward your career goals and hold you accountable. The relationship is in fact built on mutual trust.
- To ask you questions and share observations that you have never thought of.
- To cause you to reflect, which is often difficult in today's hectic business world.
- To assist you in navigating the political sand traps in your organization. Let's face it, every company has some politics.
- To help you escape a short-term perspective. Career planning involves taking long-term views of your aspirations.
- To be a *good detective*. A mentor will probe to discover the *real business* issue you are dealing with, rather than focus on the symptoms.
- To encourage you to have an insatiable curiosity about life and foster an unrelenting quest for continuous learning.

Life is a journey and mentors act as air traffic controllers in guiding employees to a safe landing.

Tales from the front lines

Mentor with Care and Candor

In late 1980 I recruited a recent MBA graduate who had majored in human resource management and economics. By definition, he was very intelligent, had an effervescent personality and was committed to his career in the human resources profession.

I assigned him to the director of compensation and benefits. Although he did not report to me directly, we interfaced frequently during various meetings and he worked with me on specific projects. This young man always completed his assignments on time and had a maturity beyond his years. He displayed good judgment.

In order to showcase him, I would bring him to executive committee meetings and from time to time have him make a presentation to the senior staff. I watched his progress very carefully and was keenly aware that we had an employee with great potential and a *can do* attitude.

After his first year of employment, I asked him to come into my office. He sat down on the couch across from my desk and thought he was there to get a new project to work on. I said, "Mark, would you like to be a senior vice president of human resources one day?" His eyes got very big and he said, "Oh yes." I said, "Okay, I am offering to be your mentor and support your career aspirations."

I stood up and asked him to sit behind my desk. After a little encouragement, he sat down. I took a seat on the couch. I queried him as to how it felt to sit in my chair. He said that it felt pretty good. I then asked the following question, "What are you willing to do to achieve your career objectives?" When he got a serious and painful look on his face, I said, "You don't need to answer now. Think about it over the next week, and we will meet again."

A week later he asked to meet with me and said, "John, I thought about your question and would like to share my response." I said, "I am all ears."

This bright individual said, "I am willing to work hard, to learn and to take on difficult tasks." He added that his father told him to listen to me.

I said that mentoring involves asking probing questions and that I would be pleased to be his mentor. I committed to help him utilize his God-given talents.

At this juncture I asked the following question, "Who is in the office the latest each day?" His quick response was, "You are."

"Who is here almost every Saturday," I asked, and he answered, "You are."

After a pause, I asked him, "Do you think I work these hours because I don't want to go home to my family?" He answered, "No, we have an awful lot of work in this department given the companies we have acquired, sales integrations, union negotiations and recruiting."

My instant response was, "You are correct."

At this point I shared with him that my father had come to America from Sicily with very little education. He worked two jobs to support the family and instilled a strong work ethic into me and my siblings. I hastened to add that I did not expect him to work the hours I worked. I told him it has been my experience that employees are compensated for the job they are assigned to do, but they are promoted by expanding their job and asking for additional duties.

I asked if what I shared with him made sense. He said, "Yes." I delivered my message in order to challenge him.

It was fun to watch him change his work habits. Before I started mentoring him, he would arrive at the office a few minutes before eight and depart at five which are normal corporate hours.

After I challenged him, he would come into my office to ask to assist me with projects, and from time to time would work a half day on Saturday. The change in his behavior was professional and refreshing. Over the next few years I promoted him twice. Today he is the director of human resources for a very large company and held in high esteem.

Mentoring involves displaying care and candor. You must provide supportive and objective communication to the individual being mentored.

I hasten to add this was also a very meaningful relationship for me as well.

Chapter 7

Are You Learning?

The highway called life is filled with the pursuit of joy, happiness and fulfillment. It is important to contemplate which roads we should navigate on this heady journey. The question is, how do we get to the desired destination? I submit to you that one of the compasses we should utilize is the power of learning.

Perhaps the first safety check we need to make is our own attitude concerning learning. Without it, we can become so engaged in the day-to-day battle of survival (given today's pressure-cooker business environment) that we do not take time to learn.

As adults we have accumulated a foundation of life experiences: joys, sorrows, wins, losses and knowledge. Hopefully as we age, all these result in the much sought after goal of wisdom. However, we can be so results-driven and consumed with achieving the goal that we miss the opportunity to learn from the experience. To quote President John F. Kennedy, "Leadership and learning are indispensable to each other."

> Effective leaders should see themselves as both learners and teachers.

Leadership and learning are members of the same family. Like a steady breeze that fills a sail causes movement toward a destination, focused leadership can inspire others to head in a certain direction. Scottish writer John Buchan said, "The task of leadership is not to put greatness into people, but to elicit the greatness that is there already."

Effective leaders should see themselves as both learners and teachers. Adults need to see a reason to learn and it has to be applicable to their work or responsibilities, in order to believe. Given the ever-changing landscape of today's business world, there certainly is ample reason to change and grow.

Child's Play

One of the keys to being a life-long learner is to look for opportunities to learn. Seek out the road signs.

You can start in your own home. I marvel how children learn. They are inquisitive. Adults tend to lose this quest for learning over the years. Unlike children, adults seek to work in comfortable and predictable boundaries. A sudden change that used to delight us when we were kids puts our guard up now. Children have no fear of learning, while many adults do.

Children look to play in the rain and the mud. They splash and find new games to play. In the business world, it is the leader's role to reduce the fear of getting all wet and to make employees work with unmitigated enthusiasm— and to enjoy the thundering rain in the world of business. What is the fear factor in your organization?

We have all been told that leadership is not child's play. During our careers, we learn leadership lessons from teachers, parents, mentors, friends and influential business leaders. So why not children?

Without a doubt, children are quite honest. Kids tell it like it is, how they feel and how they want things. While some of their communication can be quite embarrassing and brutal for their parents, without doubt their communication is genuine.

What can leaders learn from children? Do we tell it like we witness or feel it, or do we sugarcoat or window-dress our communications? The fact is that most people can indeed handle the truth. The truth shall set you free

The games children play are an element of their imagination, which leaders tend to neglect because of their obsessive focus on movement, the road ahead and the rear-view mirror. Adults respond to an issue with "Why?" while children ask the important question, "Why not?" There is a difference between movement and motivation.

How sweet it is to see children take risks, oblivious of their level of competence or incompetence. Caught in the rain, they soak in the cool wetness and take the chance of catching a chill. Another opportunity to learn.

When we list the traits of children, what words come to mind?

- Open
- Trusting
- Loyal
- Intuitive
- Responsible
- Dedicated
- Competitive
- Collaborative
- Excited
- Adventurous
- Challenging
- Moral fulfillment
- Fun-loving
- Accepting of others
- Value differences in others
- Creative
- Determined
- Dreamers
- Inventors
- Fearless
- Hopeful
- Affectionate

It makes sense to hold leadership accountable for this profile. Perhaps this will challenge some hardened leaders. When is the last time you laughed or sang at work?

A Learning Organization

Developing a culture that values creativity and encourages innovation is imperative to an organization that desires to *learn* and generate new ideas of products.

Learning involves:

- Providing employees with a challenge.
- Providing freedom to innovate.
- Providing the resources needed to innovate.
- Encouraging diversity of perspectives and backgrounds.
- Providing encouragement.
- Providing the organization with care and support.
- Having fun. (Can you believe it?)

As we stay on the path of life, we follow our natural instinct to learn and to grow. A learning organization is the breeding ground for fresh views of ourselves and of others.

I believe when we stop learning, psychologically we start to die. So learn each day and teach each day.

Tales from the front lines

Learning and Preparation

Over the past 35 years or so, I have conducted hundreds, if not thousands, of seminars, training sessions and management development programs in both the United States and internationally. It is not uncommon at the end of these events for an attendee to approach and inquire how I learned my presentation skills and the ability to be an effective trainer.

I take a deep breath, look the person in the eye and say, "If you really are interested, it is a long story." They answer, "John, I would really love to hear it." Then I say, "Here I go."

In the early '70s, I worked at Monroe Automotive Equipment in the human resource department and reported to a gentleman by the name of Larry B. Meares. He was my boss, leader, mentor and trusted friend. Early in our relationship, Larry asked me to assist him in developing a training program for supervisors who worked in the Monroe manufacturing plants.

For several weeks, we put in many hours writing a manual that addressed the functions of management, leadership, communication skills, discipline (to correct and not punish) and effective listening skills. Once the manual was completed, it was printed and bound. We developed a schedule so we could travel to all the manufacturing facilities to present this material.

I approached Larry on the first trip and asked him which section of the program he wanted me to present. He said, "John, I want you to know all the material and be prepared to discuss any section that I ask you to do

"I am learning all the time. The tombstone will be my diploma," said the late Eartha Kitt, a legendary American singer, actress and cabaret star.

Only the soul that learns experiences joy.

When you drive home after a 10- or 12-hour day, ask yourself the question, "What did I learn today?"

when we visit each plant." I can tell you that I spent many stressful hours making outlines and rereading the material in order to properly prepare.

On a Sunday afternoon, we traveled to Hartwell, Georgia, to be ready for a 7 a.m. Monday training session. I was eager, nervous and slept little, anticipating my first training session. After the plant manager introduced us, Larry stood up to discuss the outline for the three-day session. Much to my dismay and frustration, he taught the entire program without once calling on me. I was frustrated and candidly angry. I did learn from his presentation and took copious notes as I sat there for three days.

About a month later, we traveled to Arkansas to present a similar program. Once again, the plant manager introduced us and Larry kicked the meeting off. This time he said, "John Passante will conduct the entire three-day session" and promptly walked out of the classroom. That night at dinner, we had a very frank conversation and Larry said, "John, I knew that I caused you discomfort when we went to Georgia, but I wanted to teach you a lesson about the importance of preparation." Additionally, he said, "I asked you to teach the second session because I knew you could handle the presentation and I knew you were prepared."

I learned a great deal from Larry about involving others when you conduct training and the importance of being prepared at any moment to speak on a particular subject. I am indebted to Larry for his mentorship and encouragement and the impactful learning experience he gave me, as well as his faith in me. He taught me to emphasize why training was being conducted, to respect that we all learn differently and to allow participants to experience what they are learning. Most of all he demonstrated that we learn together and that was fun.

The Human Side

Chapter 8

Helpful Hints for Soul Searching

The success of any business depends on the quality of its people. Typically during an hour-long interview, human resource professionals are expected to find out as much as possible about prospective employees without violating their individual rights. Interviews are like leads in newspaper articles. It's up to you to find out who, what, when, where and why.

A resume can answer most of the standard questions about educational background and work experience, but how do you find out about the soul of an individual? Is he or she a caring person, a team player, a role model? Does the candidate possess leadership qualities?

> **Have more success in your *soul searching.***

By having in mind a clear picture of the attributes you are seeking in a candidate, you will have more success in your *soul searching*. The answers to the following questions can help you focus on your search.

1. **Support.** Is being treated with understanding, kindness and consideration important? Does the candidate need to be encouraged?
2. **Conformity.** Is the candidate more comfortable conforming to the environment rather than being a little different? Is doing what is socially correct, accepted and proper important?
3. **Recognition.** How much recognition does the individual need? Does he or she need to be looked up to in order to feel important?

4. **Benevolence.** Does the individual truly care about others? Is helping those less fortunate important?

5. **Independence.** Must the individual do things his or her way, or is there some flexibility?

6. **Leadership.** Does the individual love power, abuse power, share power? Does he or she manage or lead?

7. **Practical-mindedness.** Is *getting his or her money's* worth important to the individual? Is he or she careful with money and possessions? Does the individual do things that will pay off?

8. **Achievement.** Does the individual like to work on difficult or challenging problems? Has he or she set the highest standards of accomplishment?

9. **Variety.** Is it important to do things that are new and different and to have a variety of experiences?

10. **Decisiveness.** Is it important to have strong, firm convictions or to come to a decision quickly, then stick to it?

Tales from the front lines

Tugging at My Heart Strings

While working in Toledo, Ohio, in the early '80s for a Fortune 500 conglomerate, I was instrumental in instituting a management development program. The concept was to recruit young, bright, achievement-oriented individuals and expose them through a formal training program to the various elements of the corporation. For example, the candidates would spend time in finance, marketing, sales distribution, manufacturing and human resources over a two-year period. At the end of this development program, they would be placed in a department that matched their talents and the needs of the company. In effect, we were grooming future leaders.

In this process, I interviewed a very articulate and energetic 20-year old who had an associate degree in marketing and was going to school in the

11. **Orderliness.** Does the individual have well-organized work habits? Are things done according to schedule and are matters kept in their proper place?

12. **Goal orientation.** Does the individual have a specific goal and know where he or she is going?

So as you embark on your next search assignment, please bring to mind that a key ingredient for any executive is they must have *SOUL*—Sincerity, Openness, Understanding, and Loyalty.

Sincerity involves listening to employees concerns and showing empathy. Openness is creating a culture that encourages and fosters new ideas. Understanding means to value and celebrate differences. Loyalty is sticking by employees in both good and bad times.

The key to effective executive selection is to look for brains, a heart and clearly a soul.

evenings to complete a four-year degree. Although he did not meet all of the requirements for the management development program, I was taken with his passion and keen desire for growth and learning. I asked him to return for a second interview so that he could spend time with me and other key executives. Their feedback was very positive, but we continued to interview more candidates.

A week later at approximately 8:15 a.m., my secretary came into my office and told me this young man was on the phone. I asked her to transfer the call. He inquired as to his status, and I told him he was being considered along with other individuals. One week later, again on a Monday morning, he called to further express his interest and convey why we should hire him. Once again, I explained the interview process was continuing.

I must admit that I was impressed with his persistence.

The following Monday at exactly 8:15 a.m., he called again. I will never forget what he said to me. "Mr. Passante, do you remember when you were 20 years old and you really wanted a job and for someone to give you the opportunity to prove yourself?"

His statement touched my heart, and I really liked the cut of his jib and character. I told him to call me back in an hour. I walked down the hall and spoke with the chief financial officer and shared my impressions of my encounter with the candidate. We both laughed, concluded that we really liked this man's chutzpah and called the young man back that day and hired him!

This individual clearly demonstrated that he had heart, desire and soul. The postscript to this adventure is that he turned out to be an exemplary employee; he completed his undergraduate degree and went on to get his masters. He is now a chief finance officer for a Fortune 500 Company. There is no substitute to listening to another person's soul.

Chapter 9

The Character of Character

Reflect on your greatest heroes and heroines, your most inspirational role models. If you are blessed, the list includes your parents. Perhaps it also includes a great teacher, professor, coach and your first *real boss*, manager or leader who inspired you.

Leaders encourage us to grow and test our limits, and they provide us with challenges and nourishment for our minds and spirits. Leaders stay the course regardless of the intensity of the storm (a bad financial quarter, increased competition or quality issues). They serve as a beacon of hope for all of us.

We all live in a world overloaded with information, noise, stress and uncertainty. Yet we tend to react positively to challenges and to travel a life journey toward achieving our goals as well as keeping the internal fire of hope and joy alive in us and in others. True leaders travel with us. They shelter us, protect us and, yes, push us to be better. A true sign of character.

> Character is the sum total of lifelong habits.

When I think of the word character, many things come to mind. As I recall, my father many times shared with me the importance of being a person of character, which he defined as having integrity, being a person of your word and being a man of principle.

Character can be defined as an aggregate of traits, features, moral and ethical qualities and one's reputation. Character is the sum total of lifelong habits.

All good leaders are fallible and must engage in *self-talk*, which is the act of introspection and self-evaluation. Self-talk is a positive trait in character development that helps us grow and develop as a person and as a leader in order to make a contribution to the society in which we operate. Especially in how we interact with family, friends, and those who cross our career path.

The great philosopher Aristotle stated that character entails:

- Courage
- Temperance
- Generosity
- Magnificence
- Friendliness
- Wit
- Justice

From a leader's perspective, character means conducting yourself as a role model, embodying the principles of truthfulness and fairness, acting as a person of virtue and earning the trust of others.

Character is an ever-evolving attribute in each of us, and it is incumbent on us to nurture this asset throughout our lives. As a leader, it is essential that character be considered in every decision-making process.

A person of authentic character is an individual with the following characteristics:

- Consciousness
- Openness to experiences
- Humility
- Non-judgmental
- Constantly putting himself or herself in the shoes of the other person

A leader of character practices humility each day, recognizing it is essential to building trust and encouraging others to collaborate.

A leader of character is, indeed, the North Star that we all seek to follow—a person of value and virtue.

The character of leadership is embodied in the notion that if you take care of your employees by doing the right things, they will indeed take care of you.

Remember your employees are your internal customers who greatly influence relationships with your external customers. This is perhaps a simplistic concept, but why is it not practiced more?

The fact is we all have character. They key is to develop it so that we are able to live in a holistic way. It is interesting to note that we tend to judge ourselves by our intentions and others by our judgment of their character.

Leaders demonstrate their character in many ways through their choice of words, reactions to stressful situations when their ego is under siege and, above all, their behavior when under fire.

As a life-long student of human behavior and leadership, I feel the most important characteristic of *character leadership* is to show respect for the dignity of each person's humanity. Respect is the foundation on which relationships are built and maintained, both in professional life and in personal relationships. Being a leader of character requires great courage. It demands leading with integrity and principle, refusing to water down your values or those of the organization.

> Being a leader of character requires great courage.

Character leaders are driven by a quest for personal authenticity and the belief that we all have a natural desire for healthy self-fulfillment. Authentic leaders are the same person in every circumstance. They encourage others to be authentic and to be responsible for the choices they make. Living an authentic life involves striving to determine life's meaning and seeking our purpose in life. Character leaders assist us in this discovery process.

Here are specific traits of character leaders that I have observed:

Curious

■ Character leaders have an insatiably curious approach to life and an unrelenting quest for continuous learning. In return, they stoke the flame in each of us. They also ask great questions that engage us in thought, thus broadening our views of the business world.

Knowledgeable

■ Character leaders have a commitment to test knowledge and to share their experiences with others. They are quite persistent and have a refreshing willingness to share their mistakes. They are almost humble in their use of the power and authority entrusted to them. They help us learn and find wisdom in our experiences. Leonardo da Vinci said, "Obstacles do not bend me" and "Every obstacle is destroyed though rigor."

Creative

- Character leaders encourage others to utilize their imagination, to be playful yet disciplined, and to be iconoclastic yet traditional. It is more than okay to walk on the creative side of the street. As I look at the industry I've worked in for so many years, the automotive aftermarket, I see the creative ideas and products that influence the American motorist on a daily basis. We all need to look for and find the time for those *aha* moments. Being inspired allows us to dream more than others think is practical. The pressures of today's business world leave precious little time to think, let alone be innovative. Character leaders help us find the time and stay in the moment.

Trusting

- Character leaders display a keen willingness to lead by being vulnerable. They let go of control and power. They show trust in others and involve them in the challenges of the day.

Emotion

- Character leaders show emotion. It is impossible to be authentic without showing emotion. Honest anger is a good thing, if it is directed at a situation and not a person. Expressing anger is a lot different than acting in anger.

Open Minded

- Character leaders guide us to keep an open mind during times of uncertainty. This unlocks our creative and innovative potential. Does your organization nurture a culture that embraces uncertainty, paradox and ambiguity? In others words, is change encouraged? There is always conflict when creativity is introduced.

Futuristic

- We all look to character leaders for their view of the future. It is paramount that leaders articulate *their vision* of what lies ahead. Employees have dreams and aspirations. The character leader articulates the future by blending the three distinct aspects of organizational purpose—mission, culture and value proposition. This is the essence of character leadership.

Mission Minded

- Character leaders ensure that the right/difficult questions are being asked. The questioner will not be punished for rising to the issue.
- They create a culture of learning and questioning – and understand that mistakes and risk-taking are key parts of the road to success.
- They are not afraid of creative tensions in the organization and help others embrace the paradoxes of life.

Character leaders demonstrate a passion for inspiration and wisdom and seek to eliminate fear and uncertainty in the organization. They earn the right to be trustworthy every day, to indeed be a beacon of light in today's business storm. The Latin words facta, non-verba sum it up best: "Deeds Not Words!"

Tales from the front lines

Doing the Right Thing

I had the good fortune of working with and for people who exemplified the essence of character. The late Larry W. McCurdy, president and CEO of MOOG Automotive for many years, was a man I respected and admired. He walked the walk and talked the talk. He defined what a man of character was.

Shortly after I joined MOOG, we had a difficult year and there was a great deal of pressure from the board of directors to cut costs. It was suggested that we reduce our head count, cut salaries/wages and reduce benefits. On a wintry Saturday morning, I walked into Larry's office. He became emotional which was unusual for him because he always displayed a calm, cool and thoughtful demeanor.

He looked me in the eye and said, "John, we've got to reduce costs, but I am not going to do it on the heads of our employees. They have worked too hard and don't deserve to be punished due to poor market conditions. We need to be creative and find ways to reduce expenses."

My response was, "I agree 100 percent. Let's get together with a task force, review the costs and find a way to reduce expenses."

After an 80-hour week, we were able to develop a plan that reduced marketing costs, distribution costs, travel and advertising. Not one employee lost his or her job in the process. It took great character for Larry to resist the pressure from the board of directors to lay off employees He stood by his principles and did not equivocate. That is a lesson I shall never forget, and Larry McCurdy is in my daily prayers.

Chapter **10**

On the Count of Three—Let Go

As we travel this thing called *life*, we experience many wonderful things (emotions, love from our parents, brothers and sisters, support from family members, teachers and friends). In our work environment, we are hired by companies that train us. We report to leaders who show a keen interest in nurturing our abilities and assisting us in achieving our career goals. All of this contributes to our sense of well-being.

As the old saying goes, "It is easy to be nice to someone when they are being nice to you!"

Of course during our life we encounter people who offend us, others who belittle us in the classroom and a bully boss, so-called friend or loved one who betrays us. Oh, man, does it hurt. Thus, we start collecting bad feelings. (We all love to collect things, right?) I call it emotional baggage. This leads to holding a grudge. I am not sure, but I think the Sicilians invented the *evil eye* and the lifelong grudge.

As human beings, we also collect regrets, which we feel a sense of guilt about. We keep them stored neatly in our brains. These negative feelings take a toll on us. They drag us down, influence who we are as a person and as a leader. Additionally, they spill over to all our relationships.

Grudges are formed because we took a risk and shared things with a friend that we trusted. Then they let us down. It is indeed proper to feel resentment. The critical questions are: When can you let go? When is it time to get over it?

Holding a grudge toward another human being is like drinking poison and expecting the other person to get sick.

Grudges eat away at us, cloud our judgment and suck the joy out of us. They tend to stay with us like the flu. They shift our attention from the people and things that are important to us. When we hold a grudge we are less likely to view the world around us as positive. In order to heal, we must let go of the grudge. Try it—you'll like it!

Reflect on a current positive relationship that you have, and one that is being influenced because you cannot let go of the past.

> In order to be an effective leader, you cannot dwell on the problematic relationships in the past.

Every leader and human being has choices when it comes to dealing with people who have harmed them in some way. We have all heard about Job (from the Bible) who chose to forgive.

In order to be an effective leader, you cannot dwell on the problematic relationships in the past. Your professional happiness or fulfillment is determined by your ability to understand and collaborate with others.

It is also important to engage in self-reflection and determine if the people you lead have any reason to hold a grudge against you. Leaders have power. It is important not to abuse this power and not to take advantage of employees.

Here's a quick quiz:

- Do you listen with concern and compassion?
- Do you take it personally when an employee disagrees with you—with facts?
- Do you resent it when one of your staff has a better idea than you do?

Leaders depend on others to support the objectives of the company. It is paramount that the needs of the leader and employees are both met.

It is quite interesting that holding a grudge hurts you more than the other person. It is controlling. It controls our emotions.

Katherine Piderman, Ph.D., staff chaplain at Mayo Clinic in Rochester, Minn., writes that " … forgiveness is a decision to let go of resentments and thoughts of revenge. Forgiveness is the act of untying yourself from thoughts and feelings that bind you to the offense committed against you. This can reduce the power these feelings otherwise have over you, so that you can live a freer and happier life in the present."

The past is the past, so like a bad cold, get rid of it. It cannot hurt you anymore unless you allow it to.

Each day of our lives we should strive to:

- **Listen.** Show that we care and respect the person speaking.
- **Learn.** We learn by active listening. Carefully analyze the words of the speaker and seek the true meaning behind the words. Read each day and learn.
- **Laugh.** A good, hearty laugh is better than medicine. There is more good in life than bad. Most people in our lives are trustworthy. See the humor in things, encourage others to laugh.
- **Love.** Tell the people that you love that you love them. They may not know that you love them. Love your work and take pride in what you do. Love others who are struggling in life and offer to help them.

Let go! Each day is a gift. Forgive yourself and forgive others. Invent the future and learn from the past. Forgive people who do not deserve to be forgiven. Wow! (How about that?) That is a true sign of letting go. You will feel better as a result of it.

The more we care for the happiness of others, the greater our own sense of well-being becomes.

The Dalai Lama said it well, "Cultivating a closed warm-hearted feeling for others automatically puts the mind at ease."

Tales from the front lines

The Messenger Does Indeed Get Shot

I grew up in a Sicilian family, so I have firsthand experience with the concept of holding a grudge and revenge. I am sure most Sicilians feel they invented the emotion of holding a grudge.

It was painful for me to watch family members not speak to each for over 30 years. Then when the person passed away, there were tears and disappointment that no reconciliation between the parties had taken place while the person was alive. What a waste of negative emotion!

During my business career, I witnessed the negative impact that a grudge can have on an individual's career, self-esteem and, in many instances, family. As the old saying goes, the messenger does from time to time get shot and some leaders try to get even.

One can never be an effective leader by holding on to the past. The challenge is to let go and hold on to the future. The past is just that … the past! Let it go so it does not hurt you. By living in the past we mortgage future relationships and undermine trust.

Presidents and CEOs do indeed have egos, and of course always want to be in control. I vividly recall a middle manager who challenged the CEO at a meeting. The CEO reacted in an aggressive and accusatory manner by striving to prove the employee wrong, even though everyone in the room was confident that the employee's analysis and recommendations were 100 percent correct.

Additionally, I attended business dinners, sales meetings and cocktail parties and witnessed an employee, after his or her second cocktail, get the CEO in a corner. With great bravado they told the CEO what he or she was doing wrong and how to run the company.

The fallout from these instances was often a form of revenge. The CEO would call me into his or her office to explain why the person had to be let go. Or the CEO would articulate that the employee displayed poor judgment, therefore limiting his or her career in the company.

We all have human frailties and have said and done things that we may later regret. As an executive coach, I encourage those I work with to live with high standards, look for the best in others and look in the mirror. Regrets can be transformed into revitalization of wisdom and enlightened leadership. Forgiveness is a critical part of leadership.

Forgiveness is the best medicine for diminishing regrets and grudges. It is the visionary leader who looks for the good in others, sees the big picture and doesn't try to get mad or even. Rather, this leader is a positive architect in building mutually beneficial relationships. He or she intellectually and emotionally understands that grudges and revenge can kill us and that learning to forgive is not only good medicine but the true definition of leadership and character. In order for any of us to be forgiven for past mistakes and judgments, we have to learn to forgive.

The Human Side

Chapter 11

Ownership and Accountability

As shocking as the financial market meltdown we witnessed in 2008 was, the lack of accountability demonstrated by some of these company leaders was even more distressing. Sadly, most failed to take ownership for the difficulties that happened during their watch.

True leaders take personal or professional liability *after* the fact, determined by action or responsibility. Accountability for actions assumes a leader is willing to be held accountable for the expertise and capabilities that were placed in them by others.

I think you would agree that the leaders who have made a difference in your life sought out ownership and accountability. As challenges arose, they put up their hands and said, "I will take that project on, I will resolve the difficult issue with an upset customer, I will stay the course in times of challenge and uncertainty."

As you grow in your own leadership skills and establish personal development goals, I urge you to seek ways to become more accountable.

Why It Pays To Increase Your Accountability

In today's economy with shrinking head counts, managers do not have time to look over their employees' shoulders. They need people who will get the job done right the first time. View your job from an ownership perspective. It will give you meaning and a clearer picture of your contribution to the company. You will have a better idea of how your efforts support the overall company objectives. This in turn can help motivate you to do a better job. Accountability builds personal pride.

By being accountable, you can earn and engender the trust of your boss and co-workers. In time, this supports your career development.

What Business Needs Today

Leaders are looking for employees who seek more responsibility. Let me enumerate some of the qualities they search for:

- **Dependability.** Can your boss count on you 100 percent? Managers increasingly rely on professionals to keep strategies on track and within budget. By meeting all of your obligations efficiently and on time, you earn a valuable reputation for dependability.
- **Good Judgment.** Are you known for making good decisions? Leaders need employees who exercise sound judgment. Make sure you gather all relevant information and take a look at issues from your manager's and customer's perspective before you act.
- **Problem Solver.** Are you willing to correct a mistake, even if it wasn't your fault? Rather than pointing fingers when errors occur, focus on solving the problem. Then investigate to identify what went wrong and how similar situations can be avoided.
- **Trusted Source.** Be a truth teller. The truth is the glue that holds the company together! Come forward when issues arise, and communicate both good news and bad news on a timely basis. And be sure to be a *fact-based* truth teller.

Becoming More Accountable and a Rock Star

Want to build your accountability quotient, and your manager's trust in you? Here are some actions that can elevate you to *rock star* status within your company:

- **Make deadlines a priority.** Work with your manager to set realistic timeframes on projects. Then make sure you always meet your deadlines. If for reasons beyond your control a project is running late, let your boss know as soon as possible, work out a new schedule and show action.
- **Complete the circle.** Make sure objectives stay on track from start to finish. If you encounter setbacks during the process, take the lead in seeing that they are resolved and show creativity.

- **Keep in mind the chain of accountability.** You're accountable to your manager, who in turn is accountable to his or her boss. Always be aware that your mistakes reflect poorly on your supervisor, and on the flip side, your successes make him or her look good. The more you can make your manager shine in front of others, the more valuable and respected you will be.

- **Let the buck stop with you.** If co-workers or clients have trouble finding help, try to point them in the right direction or find a solution for them, even if the matter doesn't involve you. By lending a helping hand you will develop a reputation as the person who gets things done. See yourself as a teacher.

- **Polish your projects.** Try to make your work as accurate as possible before it reaches others. Sometimes it helps to put written communications such as memorandums, emails and reports aside for a few hours before proofing them again and sending them on. You will be able to catch errors that you might otherwise miss.

Successful people show more self-discipline than others because they have formed good habits. They are organized, never miss deadlines and demonstrate persistence. Overall, they always maintain absolute integrity and show uncommon commitment!

Join the Circle of Accountability

To earn the trust, respect and confidence of your supervisor or leader, become a dependable resource. Be a person that seeks out obligation. Execute your objectives on time and within budget. Enhance your reputation as someone that *gets it done*.

> Join the circle of accountability and exceed the expectations of your customers, peers and leaders.

To differentiate yourself from the rest of the pack, join the circle of accountability and exceed the expectations of your customers, peers and leaders. Collaborate and build supportive trusting relationships with them. Act like a winner and make a positive contribution each day.

Tales from the front lines

Earning the Right to be Accountable

When I worked at MOOG Automotive in the early '90s, I was asked to negotiate a contract at a unionized plant in Texas. I discussed my authority parameters with my boss, President Larry McCurdy, including how much budget I was authorized to spend in order to get a signed contract. Larry said to me, "John, do not increase wages and benefits by more than 3 percent." I stated that I understood my marching orders.

About two months before the contract expired, we started negotiations. Joining me on MOOG's negotiating team was the director of labor relations (who reported to me), the vice president of operations and the local plant manager. The union had eight people, including the international union representative. During the two months of negotiations, we made progress, but I always saved wage and benefit increases for the last week of the negotiations. Otherwise, we would never get the concessions we needed.

When you negotiate a union contract, the pressure always increases the closer you get to the contract expiration date. During the last week of the contract, we negotiated at least ten hours a day, and in fact, made progress. The union worked with us and we eliminated eight job classifications, which gave the company greater flexibility to move employees from one job to another to meet the production demands for our products. We also agreed on new safety and health issues.

On the last day of negotiations, we started to work on wages and benefits. As you might expect, the union sought major increases. The MOOG team communicated the need to control costs in order to compete. We thought the union employees were paid fairly. At times the negotiations became both heated and quite emotional, but never personal. Both sides worked hard to maintain a professional decorum.

We began the last day at 8 a.m., broke for lunch and dinner, and at midnight we were still at it. Frankly, we were getting drained and tired.

At 2 a.m. the union gave us their final *final* offer. I called a caucus and told the union to give us a half an hour. We went to my room to review the union's last stand. After running the numbers, their proposal would have cost MOOG Automotive an additional 3.4 percent, which was above the budget I was authorized to grant.

After negotiating for 19 hours none of us were very sharp so I called the vice president of finance at home, apologizing for waking him at that hour. Glen was always an outgoing and can-do guy. He said, "John, no problem. How can I help you?" I asked him to check my math to ensure that the calculation of a 3.4 percent increase in wages and benefits was correct. He got his calculator, and I fed him the numbers. He affirmed my math was correct. I thanked him and told him I was going to accept the union's final offer. Glen said, "Good luck and good night."

The company committee looked at me with great disbelief. The director of labor relations said, "John, we only have approval for 3 percent!" I told the team, "I am aware of that, but we cannot afford a strike since we are going into the peak selling season." My team was uptight, and the director blurted out, "Larry may fire us." I said, "Yes, he might, but I am not going to wake him up at 3:15 a.m.!"

With that we returned to the conference room where the union committee was waiting. I announced that I had, after great consideration and review, decided to accept the union's final offer. The union committee erupted into laughter, back slapping and jumping up and down. They shook our hands and promptly departed.

At this point it was approaching 4 a.m., and we had all been working for over 20 hours. I announced that I was going to bed and that I would call the president when I woke up. My committee pressed me as to what time that would be, and I said, "It depends on when I wake up!"

It is an understatement to say they were nervous. Of course, I did not sleep well after such a stressful day. I awoke at 7:30 a.m., took a shower and crawled to the hotel lobby for coffee. The director of labor relations was waiting for me, looking like he had been run over by a truck. He said, "John, are we going to lose our jobs today?" and I answered, "Maybe."

I quickly drank two cups of coffee to build up my confidence. When I called Larry's office, he was on a call with a key customer, so his secretary said she would have him call me back. However, she advised me that the vice president of finance needed to talk to me and said it was critical. She transferred the call to Glen's office and he said, "John, don't be upset with me but I told Larry about your call at 3 a.m. and that you had negotiated a contract which would cost the company an additional 3.4 percent." He continued, "Larry was very upset with you, but I wanted to give you an early warning." I said, "Glen, thanks for the heads up and the support."

I told the director of labor relations about Glen's comments, and I thought he would hyperventilate. A half hour went by without a return call from Larry, so I called again. I found out he was still on a call with a key customer. An excruciating hour went by and Larry finally called. My first comment to Larry was, "I understand that you are upset with me."

There was silence on the other end of the call for a second and then Larry stated with a chuckle, "John, you know I had to act upset when the head of finance told me that costs were increasing, but I understand that you improved our plant flexibility and that more than makes up for the additional costs. Please take Monday and Tuesday off next week because you have been working too hard, and I am worried about you. You did an outstanding job. Thank you for being decisive."

I quickly informed the company negotiating team of Larry's support, and then we all celebrated.

My story ended well because I had earned the right to be accountable with Larry and he trusted my judgment.

Chapter 12

Let's Get Real! Being the Authentic You

An interesting question, "Why is it so difficult to be the *real you*?" Part of the answer is that we are all conditioned early in life to fit in, please others and deny our feelings, needs and what we really want to do. It has been proven that children are the most creative people, yet the system sadly teaches them to comply. Children amaze their teachers with unusual responses to questions, display a keen sense of humor and are nonconforming as well as unpredictable and creative. All good traits in my book.

Often adults do not recognize the value of these creative children. Think about it, though—these children will become adults and can make a difference in our world.

Another question, "Why is it so difficult to be yourself?" Perhaps it is challenging to embrace our real selves because it involves taking emotional risks and the strong fear of rejection. No one wants to feel unworthy, so we play it safe. We wear a mask in order to avoid telling the truth about our true feelings. We seek validation and acceptance, and we shy away from any conflict.

> Being authentic takes courage.

All of us have had the experience of being in an important corporate meeting where the president proposes a business strategy that your experience and instincts tell you is doomed to fail. Everyone in the room supports the CEO's brilliant idea. Rather than standing up for what we believe (factually) is true, and to avoid taking on the boss and peer pressure, we go along with the crowd.

Being authentic takes courage. It is anchored in the willingness to feel uncomfortable at times. It takes being totally congruent in all we think, say and feel. It means living your values and true beliefs. It takes opening yourselves up to share who we are. (Are you scared yet?)

The path of personal leadership evokes purpose and true passions and requires letting others know what you cherish. It is the path to integrity and responsibility. At times we all feel there is *something* missing in our lives. The most successful executive feels this way, yet denies this feeling. We attempt to be someone else in order to protect ourselves and get our emotional needs met. Thus, an empty feeling is created inside us. We try to fill this hole with possessions, relationships (some unhealthy ones) or addictive substances. The answer is being you.

Authentic Leaders

Why is it important for leaders to be authentic? Employees put more trust in authentic leaders. Business relationships are more honest and fulfilling. They nurture *positive* climates for interactions—which of course is infectious and healthy. By being authentic, they set the tone for others to be authentic. How many creative ideas are missed or not shared on a daily basis in business because employees are afraid to be different and challenge the status quo?

> Employees put more trust in authentic leaders.

It takes corporate courage to buck the system, to seek new methods, to ask the right questions, to lead the way to change and to teach collaboration to the big boss. It starts with being the authentic you. Eliminate the fear, and dare to be you.

Given the headcount reductions that take place on a regular basis, employees are being asked to do more with less. This can leave some employees in a state of fear and unwilling to take risks. This makes it more paramount for leadership to foster authenticity and to communicate, as well as demonstrate, that they can *handle the truth* without retribution.

What would meetings be like if employees had no fear? What kind of things would be accomplished? What would be the effect on creativity, productivity and morale? Please note, I am talking openness with mutual respect and a focus on what is best for the business.

> "You can have no dominion greater or less than that over yourself."
>
> —*Leonardo da Vinci*

Of course we are all know that Socrates exhorted us to *know thyself*. Additionally, Maslow taught that personal authenticity is grounded in the belief that we all have a natural drive to healthiness and self-fulfillment.

In order to be an authentic leader, you must be aware of your feelings and willing to express them in words and behavior. Of course, there are risks in being genuine and authentic. That is why it is called leadership.

To be *real* involves:

- Being genuine and not hiding behind facades, roles, titles or office size.
- Having the ability to express one's true feelings.
- Taking the risk to be open and honest.
- Displaying unconditional, positive regard.
- Leading by being trustworthy.
- Believing that people have the natural desire to grow and develop.
- Being empathetic and accurate in order to better understand human behavior.
- Knowing who you are, and who you are not.
- Encouraging others to be authentic.

> What would meetings be like if employees had no fear?

Authentic leaders know who they are and act with more levels of interest, excitement, confidence and creativity. Let's face it, being authentic requires self-examination (hard work), reflection on one's values, goals, ego (the past hurts … let go of the past … live for today!), and hello, beliefs, we all have them, and rules that guide us in life.

The next step is to reject those that are not consistent with who *you really are*.

Align your actions, words and behaviors with who you are (be congruent).

Follow the path to purpose, passion, candor and trust. Treat others humanely with compassion, and establish meaningful, true relationships.

Being authentic is something I work on each and every day. As I pursue wisdom (I hear it comes with age), I seek lasting fulfillment. I have a joy in placing needs before wants, knowing when I have had enough, staying in the moment and truly appreciating the people around me. And to see the humor in life!

Each day is indeed a gift.

Start today, to be who you are. Polonius' advice to his son Laertes in Shakespeare's *Hamlet* is priceless, "To thine own self be true."

Tales from the front lines

The Real Deal

As I contemplate the concept of authenticity, I harken back to an experience I had while working for a major Fortune 500 conglomerate. The corporation was comprised of a diverse group of divisions that sold toys, automotive parts, home improvement products, baby products and heavy equipment.

The chairman of the board challenged me to develop a leadership program to identify high potential employees and conduct training with them so they would be prepared for additional management responsibilities.

Each divisional vice presidents had to identify their high potential employees and justify in writing why these individuals should be chosen. It was a serious investment of time and money by the corporation in its future leaders because the sessions involved staying in dormitories at Bowling Green State University in Ohio for three days.

The night before it started, a dinner was held in the university president's private dining room. Each divisional president and the corporate chairman spoke before dinner. I served as the master of ceremonies, and we all imparted the significance of what this group of individuals would be exposed to over the next three days.

Excellence can be attained if you care more than others think is wise,
Risk more than others think is safe,
Dream more than others think is practical, and
Expect more than others think is possible.

—Cadet Maxim

This is the *motto* of the cadets at the U.S. Military Academy in West Point and great advice for all of us to follow in our journey to be real.

We started promptly at 8 the next morning in a U-shaped classroom with 24 parties in the group. I started the session by going through the agenda and introduced the co-facilitator, who had a Ph.D. in philosophy.

To establish the tone for the training, I talked with the group about the traits of effective leaders. In my commentary, I stated that in order for leaders to be effective, in my opinion, they had to know who they are as a person … in other words … to be authentic. As you can imagine, the participants were pretty serious, and many of them did not know each other or what to expect because they were from all over the U.S. and Canada.

I told them we would go around the room and I would ask each of them to introduce themselves, give their background, education, families, hobbies, and biggest business and personal challenges. I walked around the middle of the classroom, and most of the participants were nervous, looking down at their shoes. Eye contact was minimal.

At that juncture, I said, "Let me tell you about John Passante." I shared with them that I was a first-generation American and that my father had come to the U. S. from Sicily. He always worked two jobs to support his family. My parents were divorced when I was eight or nine years old. My father frequently moved our family all over the country. In fact, I went to seven different grade schools. As a child I learned to fit in!

Although these experiences were painful, I told the group that I learned how to cope with changes at an early age. I think I shocked them with my candor, openness and the fact that I trusted them enough to bare my soul. During my presentation, there was laughter, and the group loosened up. At that point I asked a young accountant to discuss who she was, and she shared her background with all of us. The participants then became more comfortable.

It all went according to plan until we got to the vice president of finance. He was a tall young man, probably about 6'2", very articulate and obviously very bright. He went through his background and education, and spoke with passion about his family and the fact that he coached his son's little league team. Then he was quiet. About a minute went by, which is a long time during a group setting. He looked me in the eye and said, "John, I am going to talk about something I have never shared with anyone but my family."

To this day, I will never forget what this young man in his '30s had to say. With great emotion and his voice cracking, he said, "John I don't know who I am. Both my parents are up in age and in poor health. Six months ago, I was told I was adopted."

With tears running down his face, he said, "I am not who I thought I was." I am not ashamed to say that I also teared up as did many of the participants in the room. I went around and put my arm around this individual and said, "First of all, I admire your courage. You have a better understanding of yourself than do many others. You obviously are a man with a good soul."

We took a 10-minute break and then we all came back after we gained our composure. The seminar continued, and trust with the group had been established.

This young man and I became friends because of this shared experience, and he continues to be an exceptional leader, husband and father. When I think about being real, I can still see his picture in my mind's eye. He was certainly an authentic individual. Contentment in life is contingent upon being who you are and being authentic. He was, in fact, the *real deal*!

Chapter *13*

Your Attitude Is Showing!

There are many things we encounter in our daily lives that we cannot control or change, like the economy, stock market and weather. Perhaps the most important decision we make each morning is: What will our attitude be today?

Watch your thoughts, they build your habits. Watch your habits, they shape your character. Watch your character, it develops your attitude. Watch your attitude, it commands your behavior. Watch your behavior, it shapes your thoughts.

One of the most overlooked leadership attributes is that of a positive attitude. Leaders with an upbeat attitude inspire, motivate and engender confidence in others. We all face daily challenges, disappointments and setbacks. Our reactions to these events send a very strong message to others. Maintaining a positive attitude during troubling times clearly shows strong character and a conviction that the issues will be addressed and resolved. Leadership involves the power of positive thinking and the fuel of personal motivation to move an organization forward.

> One of the most overlooked leadership attributes is that of a positive attitude.

The mood, emotions and overall disposition of the leader impact creativity, job performance, decision-making, turnover, teamwork, negotiations and the culture of the company. The state of the boss' emotions affects how employees behave.

Recent research appearing in the *Administrative Science Quarterly* convincingly demonstrated that executive teams sharing the same level of positive effect (attitude) work better together.

The research further points out that teams which share a common attitude toward life are more successful. A positive attitude builds intimacy. Think about it, who wants to get close to a negative person? Why do people have bad attitudes? They fall prey to bad habits. Yes, attitudes are formed and a bad attitude is nothing more than an ingrained habit. The good news is habits can be broken.

Leaders that are self-actualized have a deep feeling of identification (are authentic) and have an appreciation for human beings in general. They feel kinship and connection, as if all employees are members of a single family. We are in this together.

Tales from the front lines

A D.R.I.V.E. Attitude

The late Larry W. McCurdy lived his life by his D.R.I.V.E. philosophy and encouraged others to adopt it.

D **DEDICATION.** Be dedicated to your family, church, school, job and friends. Be the best you can be.

R **RESPONSIBILITY.** Let your word be your bond. Take true ownership of issues and problems, and see them through to completion.

I **INTEGRITY.** Be open and honest in all relationships. Do the right thing, even if it hurts.

V **VISION.** What can you do today to influence your company and industry going forward? See the bigger picture and help create a better future.

E **ENTHUSIASM.** Each day is a gift. Live with an outlook that there are more good people and things than bad. Value differences of opinions and learn from them.

An attitude audit:

- Are you respected and likeable? Do your stakeholders have faith and trust in you? Do you build strong personal relationships?
- Do others seek your counsel, input and advice? Or, do people see you coming and run the other way?
- Are you often angry or frustrated with others who do not see things your way? If the majority of your conversations and interactions are confrontational and negative, then it is likely that you have an attitude problem.
- Do you reject change before you get the facts?

Attitudes and moods are contagious, like the common cold! Catching the leader's positive emotions (attitude) make employees feel better about their job assignment, their personal contributions and the company. Negative attitudes sap energy from all of us!

If you can assist one person each day to develop a positive attitude toward our industry and life, think how rewarding that will be for all of us.

When it comes to attitude, each of us are in the driver's seat. We see what we want to see. Look for the blessing we all enjoy and pass on the optimistic attitude.

"Everything can be taken from a man but one thing: the last of the human freedoms—to choose one's attitude in any given set of circumstances, to choose one's own way," proclaimed Viktor Frankl, a neurologist, psychiatrist and Holocaust survivor.

As a Greek friend of mine says, "May today be the best day of your life!"

The Human Side

Chapter 14

A Call for Kindness

Given the turmoil in today's business environment, it is often difficult to think positive thoughts.

Please note: I am a pragmatic business professional and realize that profits are the order of the day. My concern is the impact leaders have on their workforce, which in turn influences how employees behave at home. Negative behavior begets more negative behavior. We all tend to take our business problems home with us.

In their most recent book, "Leading with Kindness," William Baker and Michael O'Malley contend that corporate kindness positively impacts profits. They identify six traits of a kind leader—compassion, integrity, gratitude, authenticity, humility and humor.

I believe that a kind leadership approach improves morale, employee performance and retention.

Corporate kindness positively impacts profits.

Many times, CEOs have difficulty coming to grips with the need to make difficult decisions that negatively impact employees—i.e., reductions in workforce, plant closings, demotions, etc.—and executing these needed changes with empathy, and yes, kindness! Being kind is seen as a sign of weakness.

For the most part employees keenly understand the need to reduce costs. It is the approach and style of the way changes are communicated, handled and implemented that adds to the stress level of employees and their families.

75

A Call for Empathy

Now is the time for CEOs to stand up and show their true colors. There is a new cry for corporate leaders to demonstrate that they are keenly aware of the impact the current business climate has on their employees. In the truest sense, empathy is putting one's self in the shoes of others. Making difficult decisions and having empathy are not conflicting leadership characteristics. The question to probe is: Why are top executives uncomfortable showing their human side?

My experience as a senior human resource executive and executive coach for more than 35 years is that employees respect decision-makers who acknowledge and truly care about the human side of the business enterprise. In the final analysis people are indeed the answer to all business challenges. One of the dimensions of authentic leadership is leading with the heart. It takes courage to lead with the heart because one leaves the window to the inner person open, and therefore exposes the vulnerability of the fragile self to others.

> Employees respect decision-makers who acknowledge and truly care about the human side of the business enterprise.

Corporate Citizenship

Leaders articulate their vision, culture, tradition (in good times and bad times), values (profits, planet and people) and promote a sense of spirit. The goal here is to engender a strong feeling of attachment, fairness, compassion and, of course, kindness toward employees. Kindness is the foundation of a people-sensitive culture.

These challenging times might be the long overdue opportunity to change the view of *corporate* America into *working and living together* America.

Communication and Collaboration

It is incumbent that corporate leadership step up communications during tough economic times. Leaders must collaborate effectively with team members as to why reductions are necessary. It is paramount to involve them in the actions needed to protect the future of your company. It is interesting to note that in my experience, good news has many fathers, while bad news is an orphan! Timely and frequent communication helps combat the company rumor mill and encourages employees to focus on being productive.

The Essence of Life

It is important for leaders to reflect on what we all seek. It is something I call the essence of *life*. What is it? The essence of life is to obtain the truth, to utilize one's God-given talents, to make a contribution, to be dealt with fairly and kindly, to grow as a mature person and to have fun.

Given the stresses of today's business world it is easy to overlook the human element. Employees have very long memories, and they will vividly remember how they were treated during downturns. Let's face it, the reduction of your workforce has a negative psychological impact not only on the person laid off, but also on the person's co-workers. The good times will return. The free enterprise system has a bad cold, but it will get well and recover to be even stronger. We must preserve the American ethic.

The Purpose of Kindness

Kindness builds trust and reduces stress. It encourages creativity, humor and a sense of well-being. By acting in a kind and sincere manner, leaders facilitate a positive environment, encourage open dialogue and treat employees with the acceptance that they can *handle the truth*. Kindness influences attitudes, which impacts customer relations and company revenues.

> Kindness builds trust and reduces stress.

The Power of Being Understood

It has been said that to be understood is a luxury. The power of approaching life with kindness each day is that for the most part executives will be amazed at the positive reaction they receive from their employees. What we give out, we get back.

I am well aware that executives are taught to be tough. However, I submit to you that it takes more courage and self-confidence to publicly show your human side. It is okay for executives to be human. Employees are hungry for leadership that has the human touch! Leaders need to articulate that we all need each other. A great leader is subservient to his or her people. He or she leads by serving (helping) his or her employees.

The Business World Needs Leaders That Care

Without question, the world in general is crying out for more leaders who turn kindness into action. We all hope to encounter those who have found a soul-sized agenda for their lives that spreads kindness.

Tales from the front lines

Kindness, Even in Loss

When my business career started, U.S. manufacturers led the world in producing the finest quality products. To keep up with the demand, manufacturers were busy building additional facilities.

As a young manager, I was responsible for helping select manufacturing sites and taking all the necessary steps to build these new plants from scratch. In addition to working with local officials, I would interview hundreds of people, do background checks, and contact local health officials to complete physicals. Once the plant was completed, training was required.

All this activity added jobs and value to many small cities throughout the '70s and '80s. Global competition made inroads and perhaps was not taken as seriously as it should have been. By the '90s global competition was alive and well, and U.S. manufacturers found their market share and profits eroding.

Due to these business conditions, I helped close manufacturing facilities that employed more than 200 employees. This was an arduous and stressful assignment. I negotiated the closing over a six-month period and had frequent communications with the employees as to the cause of the plant shutdown. The employees understood the rationale for the decision and, of course, were anxious and saddened by losing their employment.

The Lebanese poet Kahlil Gibran once said that we should do a life's work that causes us to laugh all our laughter and to cry all our tears.

Kindness is putting yourself on the line. It builds positive energy and positive action.

I believe passionately in kindness, and so do you.

Start today to show it. Pass it on, it is contagious.

Kindness enables all of us to hope, and cope, each day!

As a gesture of support, I would schedule a Saturday training seminar for everyone who would be negatively impacted by the plant closure. The seminar taught skills for completing an application, writing a resume and preparing for an interview.

I remember one time when approximately 100 employees showed up for the Saturday session. I also invited the employees and their spouses to a dinner that night so that I could explain to the family members why the decision was made to close the plant, the services the company offered to displaced employees and our severance package. The dinner was well attended. There was a question and answer session and the mood was one of appreciation and concern. The spouses were pleased to have the opportunity to learn firsthand regarding this significant event in their lives.

The plant closure took place over a five-month period, and each month a certain percentage of employees would work their last day. Our benefits manager and I would meet with these employees who were being furloughed and present them with their COBRA benefits, 401(k) summary, pension data, severance package and a letter of recommendation.

As you would imagine, these were emotionally trying days. It was difficult to say goodbye to good employees, some of whom had worked for the company for 25 or 30 years. There would be tears and hugs and, much to my amazement, many of these individuals who lost their livelihood brought gifts. To me that clearly exemplified the kindness in people's hearts. It is a living example that when companies work hard, and show kindness and compassion (in both good and bad times), employees will rise to the occasion and teach all of us the definition of kindness.

Chapter 15

Heart and Soul

The success of any business enterprise is based on increasing profit, revenue and market share. The key elements of an organization are its product, processes, distribution, customer base, image, customer service, its ability to innovate and adapt quickly to global market conditions and the quality of its people. Obviously this is a tall order.

For those of us that toil in today's business world, I pose this question: Can and should a business have a heart and soul?

I am sure that many hard charging, bottom line driven leaders would respond to this question in a negative fashion and I can perhaps understand their point of view.

True leaders are accountable to provide direction and a creative vision of the future. With that vision, they need to view the business through a different lens. The lifeblood of any enterprise is fresh ideas that lead to innovation, which in turn drives profitability and sustains the future. In effect, businesses must continue to reinvent themselves in order to offer new products, services or processes that contribute to the long-term success of the business. Innovation is the lifeblood of any organization.

> The heart of any business are its people.

The heart of any business are its people. A company's culture either supports its people or does not.

People give the business its spirit and its freshness. They are the face of the company to its customers, investors, vendors and public. People have knowledge and opinions about your business, and the ability to influence its success. They are the heartbeat of the company. Their loyalty, commitment and recommendations are essential to long-term growth.

The factor influencing the *heart* of a living organization is touch. Heart has the ability to truly touch the customer and respond in kind to their needs. As important as the company's advertising and marketing messages are, employees are in fact the most important element of a company's image. Human beings can emote, laugh, listen and show compassion to others, while computers cannot. This is the essence of heart.

The elements of corporate *soul* are purpose, passion, courage and striving for greater achievements. Soul is the fire that motivates employees and encourages them to dream big. It fuels excitement and a feeling of belonging to something special.

Soul is the moral fiber and compass that guides the organization to exceed business objectives and to do good at the same time.

A relationship-based organization is solidly anchored in soul.

Some people say, "Come on, markets are not about morals, they are about profits." I say this is old thinking. That's a false choice.

"The great companies will be the ones that find a way to have a hold on to their values while chasing their profits and brand value will converge to create a new business model that unites commerce and compassion. The heart and the wallet. The great companies of this century will be sharp to success and at the same time sensitive to the idea that you can't measure the true success of a company on a spreadsheet," said Bono, the leader of the band U2 and a noted social activist.

> A relationship-based organization is solidly anchored in soul.

Perhaps the concept of soul and the business world appears at first glance not to be a good fit; however, upon deeper investigation and contemplation, we should be able to connect the dots.

I am firmly convinced that every organization has a soul. It is woven into the fiber of its culture. It is witnessed by the well-being of its employees, the wondrous spirit that one sees in their eyes and the enthusiasm that is in the atmosphere. Soul is a persuasive calling of being engaged in activities that make a difference.

What Will You Choose?

The book "Trust Agents" states that, "A leader with soul acts as a human artist, a person who understands the so-called 'soft skills.'"

> I am firmly convinced that every organization has a soul.

If the human side of business is so difficult, why is it called the *soft side*?

The *soft side* is indeed difficult because it influences all aspects of an employees work life and carries over to what they do at home. It influences moods, personalities, self-image, energy, pride and the ability to perform to their potential. Good leaders must understand and appreciate the *soft side* of the business.

As soul singer and songwriter George Jackson proclaimed: "You Gotta Have Soul!"

Here's how I define a company's S.O.U.L.:

S **Service**, responding to the needs of customers, employees, vendors and shareholders.

O **Open** to risk taking and change.

U **Understanding** the importance of its employees.

L **Loyal** to its associates in good times and in bad times.

Does your business have or desire a heart and soul? Perhaps now is the time for your company's 100,000-mile check-up.

Tales from the front lines

Practicing Forgiveness

One of the most rewarding aspects of leadership is when you have the opportunity to recognize performance and promote an employee. I remember working with a highly spirited, hard-charging salesman. He always went the extra mile, built productive relationships with his customer base and brought great passion to any assignment.

As a result I met with him and offered him a sales management position that required relocation. At this meeting I gave him a copy of our company's relocation policy, which was quite detailed. I asked him to read this document and get back to me.

One of my staff members came to my office the next day and said, "I need to make you aware of something. The salesman who was offered the position is bad mouthing the company's relocation policy and you personally." Of course, I was dismayed, disappointed and somewhat hurt and angry to hear this news. A day later, another employee in the company told me a similar story.

Soon the young salesman was back in my office to review the relocation policy. We spent over two hours going through each paragraph in intense detail. At the conclusion of this session, he was very pleased with what our company would do for him and his wife and thanked me.

Of course, being a Sicilian, I was tempted to share with him what I had learned about the negative comments he shared with others regarding the company and me. But I bit my tongue and swallowed hard.

The next morning as I drank my coffee, this young salesman came to my office and said he had a confession to make. "When I first read the relocation policy, I was unhappy and I spoke ill, not only of the company, but of you, and I was wrong. I did not sleep at all last night because you have been kind to me and supported me and I let you down."

I could see the stress in his eyes and on his face. After a moment of silence, I responded, "I was aware of your comments and frankly was disappointed. I chalked it up to your immaturity and your lack of business experience. Let me emphasize that I still believe in you. I hope that one day you will have empathy for a young salesperson who may make a similar mistake and that you will use this experience as a learning opportunity." This gentleman is now a vice president of sales with a large global manufacturer.

A key element of leadership with soul is looking for the good in others and practicing forgiveness. Soul involves teaching as well as caring more than others think is practical.

The Human Side

Chapter **16**

Leave the Change

As an executive coach I am often asked by presidents and senior executives, "Do you think people can really change?" Being a decisive person, I reply yes and no! Ask yourself these questions: "Can you change?" "Have you changed?" I suspect your answer is a loud yes.

It has been my experience that people transform based on life experiences. We encounter personal health issues, deaths of loved ones, illnesses, promotions, relocations, children and retirement. These events create new realities and in effect force us out of our comfort zone.

Remember, butterflies leave their *comfort zones*—the cocoon—because they feel it is safe to do so. In effect, they display courage and trust. As a leader, do your employees feel safe to venture out of their *comfort zone*?

Dan Oestreich, a reflective leadership coach states, "Is there a similar human experience like that of the butterflies? I would say not one but many. We are transformed constantly simply by growth and things happening to us. We are always dealing with new life situations, while we are losing others."

Think about this in Greek. Psyche is the Greek word for "soul," but also the word for "butterfly." We all know that butterflies do not change, they transform. We are all butterflies.

According to Bill Bridges, an internationally known speaker, author, and consultant who advises individuals and organizations in how to deal productively with change, "Transition, by comparison, is the psychological process of adapting to the change, a process that occurs in predictable emotional stages."

> Transformation is the quest for self, the journey for personal well-being.

According to a recent *Time* magazine article, "Corporate culture has long ignored the fact that we can't check our feelings at the office door." Why is it high time to be rational about emotions in the workplace?

To me transformation is the quest for self, the journey for personal well-being. It involves both the heart and the soul.

Leadership plays an important role in the transformation of individuals. The leaders that impact our daily lives:

- **Inspire us**
- **Accept us for who we are and who we can become**
- **Are committed to us**
- **Encourage us to fly … like the butterfly**
- **Do not control or trap us**
- **Listen to us, without judging**
- **Listen with both their head and heart**

In the work environment, change is indeed the watchword. Companies and employees must change in order to compete. Performance reviews would be pointless if people were not able to adapt to changes in culture, structure, leadership, etc.

Change/transformation is a two way street between the leader and the employee, with trust as a key element in the process. The leader assists the individual in recognizing the need for change by encouraging introspection. Leaders listen and guide to collaborate the passions and the desire to change. Leaders provide open and candid feedback to the employee in good and bad times. They give unconditional emotional support and encouragement throughout the process.

A paramount responsibility of a leader is to evaluate and determine if an employee is the right *fit* for the current position and for future promotions.

It is critical to ascertain if employees can change or transform their approach and thinking to a job. Will they actually do it?

To change is to grow and nourish the world around us. We have all had leaders that have nurtured us and permitted us to be *us*. They got us out of our cocoon.

Our mission now is to pass it on. Reflect on the employees in your company who need to change or transform for their own good and for the long term good of the organization.

Take the steps and show the courage to reach out to these employees and help them reach their potential. Remember, others did it for us.

Next to breathing, self-fulfillment is one of our deepest human emotional needs. It is important when a leader understands this and *feels you*. To *feel you* means the leader and his employee are communicating on the same wave link. As a result, you feel valued and truly appreciated.

In the words of Charles Darwin, "It is not the strongest of the species that survives, nor the most intelligent that survives. It is the one that is the most adaptable to change."

Challenges of various sizes and shapes occur everyday. The question is how do organizations and leaders respond to *change*? Cultures that support high performance put issues into perspective. They are performance-focused firms that stress collaboration and teamwork—in good and bad times. The key factors are common objectives, commitment to a shared vision, mutual respect and a system that mentors the best performers and works to raise everyone's performance.

> Cultures that support high performance put issues into perspective.

Both individual and organizational change/transformation are anchored in a culture of resilience.

Who are the change/transformational leaders in your organization? Perhaps every business needs an executive vice president of change. Their duties would include preparing the organization for *change* (in up and down markets), mentoring employees and assisting them to fly or grow and reinforcing a culture of resilience. This individual would help the organization learn from both successes and failures, as most companies do not do a post mortem on successes.

Tales from the front lines

Perception and Change

I once taught an executive development seminar for St. Louis University designed to expose future leaders to the concepts of perspective, change, the importance of valuing differences and becoming a champion of change. My co-facilitator was a Ph.D. with a degree in industrial psychology.

After a four-hour morning session, we had lunch and came back for the afternoon session. We broke the 40 attendees into five teams of eight. Here was the assignment: "Over the next two hours, design a program that addresses how you would implement positive change in your current company culture; be prepared to give examples and to utilize the skills and tools that were shared with you at the morning session." All teams were assigned to their own classroom so that they could work in a quiet environment without interruption. We encouraged creativity.

My co-facilitator and I were available to answer any questions but would not solve the issue for them. Additionally, we circulated between the groups to observe their behavior and monitor their progress.

I wandered into one of the classrooms to observe. Keep in mind that of the 40 attendees, only three were females. As I stood quietly in the back of the classroom, I heard one of the males in the group say to the one young lady on their team, "I think it's appropriate that the girl takes the notes."

Mind you, this was in the '90s. I wanted to fall to the floor when I heard this executive's comments. Then, all hell broke loose! The many male

I am convinced that people and organizations can change. The transformation requires self-awareness, and the mental toughness to highlight both strengths and weaknesses. It comes down to fostering strong and meaningful relationships.

Remember the butterfly!

members turned with great vigor and anger and said, "We can't believe you said that!" The people attending this seminar were from different companies so they did not work together or know each other. There was yelling and everyone spoke at once.

In order to let the group resolve the issue on their own, I quietly exited the classroom. Of course, I was quite interested to learn the outcome of this group dynamic. When I returned an hour later, the executive who had stated, "Let the girl take the notes" was the note taker. The young woman was leading the group, guiding them to resolve their challenges. The team was fully engaged and on point.

When the teams returned to the main classroom and made their presentations, I was impressed with their creativity and teamwork.

At the conclusion of the workshop, the gentleman who had made the reference to the girl asked if he could speak to the group. I said, "Certainly." Then I sat down. He walked to the head of the classroom and said, "I learned an awful lot today, and I would like to apologize to my team members and particularly to our female member. This seminar was an epiphany for me and, in effect, was a mind shift. As a result of this experience, not only have my perceptions and actions changed, but they will continue to change. This was an incredible wake-up call and a remarkable new start for me, not only as a business leader but as a human being."

People become remarkable when they start realizing they can change. That is the secret of true success.

The Human Side

Chapter 17

Lip Service or Customer Service?

The watchword at many companies is control costs (at any cost?). To meet these goals, some firms have reduced staff or shortened the hours of operation. In many cases this has negatively impacted customer service and the customer experience.

Excellence in customer service is the lifeblood of any organization. According to a Harvard Management update by Bain & Company, "Eighty percent of companies believe they deliver a superior customer experience, but only eight percent of their customers agree." What is your customer satisfaction index? Have you polled your clients for feedback?

The customer experience often seems to be ethereal, something that appears as if by magic. Think of Southwest Airlines. The good news is great customer service does not require knowledge of magical incantations; it springs from human touch (yes, human), not your smartphone. Remember, the customer is always right. It is our job to make the customer more right.

> Excellence in customer service is the lifeblood of any organization.

Commitment, responding to a client's issues and displaying empathy is what I call the customer journey. There is a danger that business today has become too internally focused. Who is the voice of the customer in your organization? It is paramount to remember that for long term success, the customer experience needs to be seen as the sum-total of how the customer engages with the company and its brand, as well as the entire arc of being a customer.

Great customer service starts with good employee morale. Do your employees feel good about what they do? Have your customer service people ever met a *live customer*? Do they clearly understand and appreciate the needs of your customer base? Do they feel good about their contributions to the goals of the company? Do they feel appreciated for the job they do? Does your company really value customer service or view it as a necessary evil? Invariably companies that care about their people are in a better position to ask them to care about their customers.

Caution:

- Never complain about customers. They pay the bills.
- In meetings, someone should be assigned to be the voice of the customer.
- Decisions should be made with the intent to support the customer.
- Even when the customer is wrong, they are right.
- Ask a customer to attend one of your company's meetings, in order to communicate his or her expectations of the company.
- When a customer is upset, it gives the organization the opportunity to show its true colors.
- Anticipate conceivable customer questions, issues and problems. Create a seamless experience that appears effortless to the customer. We all know that making something look easy is in fact hard.
- Articulate your value proposition and live up to it.

Providing a Creative Service Experience

While living in Toledo, Ohio, I befriended a gentleman who owned a service station in West Toledo. The key word here was service! The economic climate in the '70s was very robust in Toledo with employment at an all-time high. Companies like Dana, Questor, Champion Spark Plugs, Sheller-Globe, Owens Illinois and Libby Owens were recording incredible sales and profits.

- Develop a process that delivers excellence to customers—again and again.
- Develop customer metrics (with input from your customers). They will allow you to be sure your standards are being met! Leaders look for formal and informal ways to let customers tell them whether or not they're meeting their expectations.
- The company with the best customer service wins (Southwest Airlines).
- Customers seek human touch points, a supportive voice on the other end of the phone line (interactive voice response systems drive me crazy), a timely response to a voice mail and email and a creative approach to a crisis. They want a customer service professional that actually listens.

The key elements of a great customer experience are customer FOCUS.

F **Frame** the needs of your customers.

O **Organize** your company's capabilities to determine the scope of your customers' business objectives.

C **Collect** and seek data from your customers. What is their product story?

U **Understand** the true voice of your customer. Listen to gain insight vis-à-vis their concerns and opportunities.

S **Select** an action plan that generates and executes the plan to clearly address the needs of the customer.

Beware of the dominance trap: The larger your company's market share, the greater the risk of taking customers for granted. Customers are not statistics—they are people. It is our role to never stop showing that we care—with thought and positive action.

Like now, people then were busy balancing work, home, children, etc. My friend was incredibly innovative and understood the true meaning of service and how to exceed the needs of his clients.

He had five mechanics on his staff. One would come to your place of business, pick up your car and take it to the station. At the station they performed any required maintenance, tune-ups, state vehicle inspections, tire rotations or an oil change. At the end of the day, the mechanic would return the car to your place of business.

Not only had the car been serviced, but it was washed, vacuumed and air was added to any tires that were below the required level. The bill would be on the front seat of the vehicle, along with a thank you note from the owner of the station. If the car belonged to a woman, there would be a rose placed on the front seat!

When you stopped at his station for gas, you were greeted by an attendant who smiled, pumped your gas, washed your windshield and checked your oil and all your fluid levels. He even washed your headlights, and all for no extra charge! Can you get your mind around this?

My friend was busy six days a week and built an incredible reputation in Toledo. Many of his clients were with him for over 20 years. He was so successful that he retired at age 53 and now lives happily in Florida where he plays a great deal of golf.

We need to revisit our commitment to customer service. As a business professional and a consumer, I am concerned that customer service as we once knew it is either dead or has a bad case of the flu. It is time to renew our commitment to American customer service.

Excellent customer service pays off. It should be viewed as a commitment by every organization and not as a cost of doing business.

Chapter 18

The "E" in Sales is for Enthusiasm

Many medical studies indicate that happy and positive people have fewer health problems than people who are negative about life. In other words, we are what we think! When you wake up in the morning and think you are going to have a bad day—guess what? You have a bad day.

In today's business world, sales professionals have a certain amount of concerns, and yes, fears when they feel they will not make their sales goals. Chances are they are indeed right.

As human beings we many times look outside ourselves for answers. But you see, the answers are within each and every one of us.

Einstein said, "When you change the way you look at things, the things you look at change." That is powerful.

Let's look at the way we look at business today. Global competition is in fact real. Companies continue to consolidate. Customers expect more from their manufacturers and distributors. Do you see any opportunities in these business conditions? I do. Competition makes us all better.

> Your attitude sets the tone for the entire day.

Consolidation provides the ability to serve larger customers. Customer demand gives reason to excel in customer service. We see what we want to see in life.

Our attitude drives our behavior.

As you develop professionally, take a moment to reflect on how you approach your job.

There is no substitute for approaching each day with a strong sense of purpose and passion.

It has been said that our attitudes define us. Each of us are in charge of our attitudes. We all have a free will. So when you approach your daily tasks, what do you choose?

Your attitude sets the tone for the entire day.

We live in a busy and hectic world, yet there is still plenty of room for joy and fulfillment. It is solely up to each of us to decide our attitude for the day before we jump out of bed in the morning. Lay there for a few seconds and talk to yourself. Be thankful for the day and commit to yourself to make the day a positive one. Find ways to assist others throughout the day and smile more. Remember, "Each day is a gift."

Tackle challenges, business issues, etc. with a strong dose of enthusiasm.

Many years ago, I was taught "the power of enthusiasm in selling."

- **Enthusiasm is the outward reflection of an inner belief.** It reflects our belief in ourselves, our company, our product or service. Hence, it gives the prospect confidence in us and what we offer.

- **Enthusiasm reflects knowledge.** The sales professional who really knows his or her product offering radiates enthusiasm, as naturally as a stove radiates heat. Prospects naturally prefer to do business with sales professionals who know the answers.
- **Enthusiasm engenders energy**, and the energy is the power that drives the sales professionals to make the calls necessary to make the sale!
- **Enthusiasm is contagious** (like the flu)! It enables us to override our fears and strengthens our ability to overcome doubts and fears in the minds of our prospects.
- **Enthusiasm conveys a sense of self-confidence and professional commitment.**
- **Enthusiasm sells.**
- **Enthusiasm builds relationships.**

Enthusiasm is the value-add in the sales personality that makes the difference between a sales professional and a sales person.

Happy, positive and enthusiastic people live longer than negative, pessimistic people. So for health's sake, put on a sincere, happy face.

Walk on the sunny side of the street. To choose one's attitude in any given circumstance is to choose one's own way.

Have faith in the future and faith in yourself.

Tales from the front lines

Enthusiasm Carries the Day

We all have down days when enthusiasm wanes. When I do, I think of a man I knew who spent over three years (1,096 days in captivity) as a prisoner of war in Vietnam. This remarkable man lived in a hut with little protection from the elements, where the weather in Vietnam can be horrific.

Yet even with this inhumane experience in his past, my associate now approaches each day with great enthusiasm and joy!

Like many POWs, he rarely discusses how he survived physically and mentally in conditions that none of us can imagine or comprehend. One afternoon he was in a reflective mood and gave me a peek into his ordeal as a POW. He said, "I survived because we devised a way to communicate. It was a tapping system, in effect a 'tap code.' Of course, as a prisoner, we lacked social interaction and group dynamics. Plus we were brainwashed constantly."

He continued, "A wave, a wink, thumbs up or tap means a great deal when you are in solitary confinement. This helped me to stay sane and encouraged me to stay the course for another day. Some POWs gave up and would lie in their beds all day. Through our tap system (The letter A was one tap, B was two taps), we compiled an unabridged Bible from memory and appointed chaplains to help us cope." This American hero shared with me that he was once forced to kneel on a concrete floor for days.

"We found a way to bond with fellow POWs," he explained. "We deliberately broke camp rules and got locked up with other prisoners for three days, but at least we were together." What amazed and touched my heart was that this gentleman, who lived in wretched conditions with minimal care, now lives his life with pure enthusiasm.

As a POW he had a great deal of time to think. He determined that the most important things in his life were family, faith and to make a positive contribution to his country. He vowed to be a better person as a result of being a POW.

This ex-POW focused on the future when he was in captivity and dreamed each day of coming home, sleeping in a normal bed, being more grateful for people in his life and celebrating each day with tremendous enthusiasm. He is passionate about having lunch with friends (an event we all take for granted) and remembers all the good he's had in his life.

And let me tell you … boy does he celebrate! On each major holiday, he decorates his home to the nines. During the Christmas season, to say he celebrates would be a gross understatement. He begins decorating for Christmas in late October. As you drive by his home, you will see him putting up the nativity scene, Santa Claus, Rudolph and various reindeer, Frosty the Snowman, Alvin and the Chipmunks as well as angels. The entire town comes to see his display because every year he adds to it.

When you ask him about his passion for the holidays, he responds, "Well, I spent three years in a cage in Vietnam. I promised myself I would never take a holiday for granted, nor would I take any human being for granted. I live each day with as much enthusiasm that is humanly possible and hope, that by decorating my home, I cause people to smile more and to realize how grateful we all should be."

It is remarkable that this hero has no bitterness and feels his experience as a POW made him a better person. He's a clear example of enthusiasm defined.

The Human Side

Chapter 19

Is Sales A True Profession?

Quite early in my business career, I worked for a major manufacturer with a commanding brand presence in the automotive aftermarket. It was the brand of choice and the sales force was held in high regard. It was a high-octane group of hard-charging, driven individuals with a passion for customers, sales and life. They were fun loving, known to party and burn the candle at both ends. Our industry was experiencing double digit sales growth. During that period of time sales drove the business and the entire organization participated in its success.

Selling at this company was viewed as every employee's responsibility because in one form or another everyone touched and influenced the customer. The annual company sales meetings were events that would make Hollywood jealous. The awards dinner was always filled with great emotion and pride. To receive the *Sales Person of the Year Award* was a big deal

The national sales meeting not only celebrated sales achievements but also acknowledged the accomplishments of other departments in the company, like accounting, customer service and marketing. Sales success was indeed a team sport. These gatherings provided a forum to integrate all parts of the organization and to align business goals and objectives. The payoff was a greater awareness of the needs of the customer and a more collaborative organization with an appreciation for the sales process. Sales professionals tend to run on emotion and this emotion manifests into profit.

I have always had great respect for the sales profession and viewed sales as the engine that drives the company. Yet when we think of professions, sales often doesn't come to mind as frequently as do law, accounting, engineering and architecture. But in every company, a true rainmaker is a sales professional. They are individuals who see each call as a sale and a *no* to them is a *maybe*.

> I have always viewed sales as the engine that drives the company.

Some view sales people as party animals who lead an easy life, cost the company money and eat at expensive restaurants. The fact is the customers of today demand bright and analytical visionaries who are true business people with high ethical standards, strong service skills, interpersonal abilities, great listening skills and excellent technological knowledge. Today's customer seeks a sales partner.

According to the American Society of Training and Development, professional selling is, "The holistic business system required to effectively develop, manage, enable and execute a mutually beneficial, interpersonal exchange of goods and/or services for equitable value." This is an excellent standard to communicate to your sales team and your organization. Professional selling means you must learn your customer's business, find and eliminate the pain or problem they are dealing with and build trust.

Brian Lambert, Ph.D., is the leader of sales enablement and strategy at GP Strategies. He defines the three tenets of professional selling as follows:

"The focus of the sales professional centers on the human agents involved in the exchange between buyer and seller."

"Effective selling requires a systems approach, at minimum, involving roles that sell, enable selling and develop sales capabilities."

"A specific set of sales skills and knowledge are required to facilitate the exchange of value between buyers and sellers."

The definitions help to articulate and adopt a sales culture.

Larry Silvey, former chair of the automotive aftermarket management program at Northwood University in Midland, Mich., provides this perspective on sales: "I would argue that a true sales professional is every bit a professional as a lawyer, doctor or accountant. In effect, a true sales professional serves his clients, rather than sells to his clients. A true sales professional is a consultant and partner to their clients. In effect, the true sales professional is one who is an extension of a client's staff—a person who knows their client's business as well as the client and makes recommendations based on the client's needs rather than the wants of the salesperson's company."

The sales profession is in transition. Today's sales professional is a knowledgeable worker striving each day to eliminate the customer's pain, assist in inventory management, communicate product value, stay ahead of global competition and foster lifelong customer relationships.

It is time to examine our attitudes toward sales and view the function as a key element of revenue and growth. A sales professional is a customer educator, collaborative communicator, sales strategist and person who sells value and solutions. To win more business today, go after the real competition—the status quo. Help your clients move from complacency to curiosity and finally to closure.

"I have never worked a day in my life without selling. If I believe in something, I sell it and sell it hard," said author Robert Keith Leavitt.

It is time for the sales function to be viewed as an asset and not a liability. Strong branded products and a well-trained, focused and professional sales force are what make any industry great. We should be adding sales people, not eliminating them!

> It is time for the sales function to be viewed as an asset and not a liability.

Tales from the front lines

The Touch of the Sale

One of life's joys has been to meet—and develop a positive relationship with—a person of character, as well as a true, bona fide, 100 percent *character*.

Warren Ellis came into my business life when I was young and eager to learn all I could about business relationships and the magic of the profession called sales. He was a man of great passion and gusto.

When I first met Warren, he immediately reminded me of Winston Churchill. He was built like Churchill, smoked large cigars and enjoyed having an adult beverage. Warren was sneaky smart (perhaps brilliant), as was Churchill. As a child, he was an outstanding ice skater and full of tireless energy. His energy stayed with him throughout his life. I am not sure of the origin of Warren's characteristic positive perseverance.

Warren was not exactly a picture of good health. Yet in every sales meeting or sales call, he displayed incredible intelligence and emotional resilience. When a customer said no to Warren, he interpreted this as a maybe and used the experience to rejuvenate himself and those around him.

To quote Churchill's speech at the Harrow School in London, "Never give in. Never give in. Never, never, never, never—in nothing, great or small, large or petty—never give in, except to convictions of honor and good sense." This was Warren's mantra.

Warren took a liking to me and taught me to appreciate and respect sales as a true profession. His larger than life presence, coupled with his physical appearance, caused people to notice him in any social or business gathering. He asked me to accompany him to meetings with difficult customers because he said I had the ability to communicate effectively and possessed great listening skills. I appreciated his compliments but the magic that took place when we met with an angry and emotional customer was due to Warren's gift in diffusing the situation and causing people to laugh. He would turn the meeting into a positive sales call. His integrity came through loud and clear.

Although he had an ego, he would never let it prevent him from doing what was best for both the customer and the company. He was viewed as the Pied Piper because Warren had a heart bigger than his body. Very much like Winston Churchill, Warren was a human magnet with a huge abundance of charisma. He was an astute business professional who understood sales and marketing strategy, as well as the sales process.

Much like Churchill, he was a persuasive orator and would have people eating out of his hands when he spoke. Warren was proud to be a sales professional. He stepped up to the demand of his position, traveling frequently to see customers and teaching those who had the blessing of working for and with him.

I marveled at his ability to relate—on both a personal and business basis—with CEOs of large organizations as well as strangers he met at the airport, restaurant or neighborhood tavern. Warren had a keen sense of invincibility, emboldening him to pursue the next sale with supreme courage.

Much to the surprise of customers, Warren would often quote the classics in a meeting. He used both his intelligence and emotional IQ. To paint a bright tapestry of what working with Warren and his team would look like, he made the customer clearly aware of the true, positive potential of selling.

It has been said that Winston Churchill was the right man for England during World War II. Well, Warren Ellis was the right man for the sales profession. He mentored, trained and hired many employees who went on to bigger and better assignments as sales professionals due to his tutelage. We all owe a great deal to Warren for having a clear understanding of the profession called sales.

The Human Side

Chapter 20

Your Legacy is Now

The time for leaders to think about their legacy is now. Most of us view the word legacy as a term closely tied to retirement. In fact, your legacy involves forward thinking. In a broader context it forces you to focus on the impact and actions you take today.

Each individual you influence, each strategy you devise and each decision you make is part and parcel of your legacy as a leader. Your legacy is the experiences and memories that others have when they think of you.

You walk the trail of your legacy each and every day. Consider the picture you paint and the landscape you plant in how you treat others, and how you are viewed by associates, vendors, industry leaders and your community.

> Legacy is making a positive influence on others that outlasts you.

Legacy is opening yourself up and investigating your intentions. It's a self-awareness that your reputation is built and hopefully enhanced each day. The question we all must face is: What is important in life? Whatever your answer is, you must lead your life accordingly.

Walter Lippmann, an American newspaper commentator and author who in a 60-year career made himself one of the most widely respected political columnists in the world, said it well, "The final test of a leader is that he leaves behind him in other men the conviction and the will to carry on."

Legacy is making a positive influence on others that outlasts you. It is akin to a well written song or opera that is listened to often. Each time the music rings in your ears it evokes a strong appreciation and emotion.

It is paramount for today's leaders to study and learn from the past, and especially from those leaders who helped shaped the industries where they dedicated their careers.

My experience in the automotive aftermarket has taught me that without question that the brave entrepreneurs who had the vision, character and courage to start companies that kept America's cars and trucks on the road were a special breed. They literally bet the farm to start jobbing stores, warehouses and manufacturing facilities. These were family enterprises. Fathers, mothers, sons and daughters worked in the business.

Of course we all owe a great deal of gratitude to these pioneers. They gave us a rich and precious legacy that we must nurture and cherish. The leadership style of the automotive aftermarket's founding fathers and mothers was that of involvement, task orientation, pleasing the customer, watching costs and treating employees like family.

Perhaps this leadership approach is best described as paternalistic. They cared about the employees and the customer

Of course most of the firms in today's automotive aftermarket are quite large and complex. A paternalistic management style does not fit their corporate culture. The challenge is to lead with a style that engenders a commitment to your industry.

What can we learn from the legacy of past leaders?

When we think about yesterday's leaders, we should use vibrant, living verbs that speak of risk taking, passion and people who were proactive. We should envision leaders who took purposeful action and truly lived the business.

They had a strong commitment to test knowledge, through experience, persistence and a willingness to learn from mistakes. They were lifelong learners that championed change along with professional and personal growth.

The question is: What type of leader are you? What type of leader would you like to be? What can you learn from the leaders of the past?

Passing on Your Legacy

Years ago, I was interviewed for a key executive position at MOOG Automotive on a beautiful spring day. I was to meet and be interviewed by Gianluigi "Luigi" Gabetti, the chairman of Fiat, which at the time owned MOOG. Our interview was at the Pierre Hotel in New York City.

Luigi treated me warmly and with a lovely Italian accent. He reviewed my resume and background and we talked for over an hour. At that point Luigi looked me in the eye and said, "I have no power or authority to hire you. That decision is up to Mr. McCurdy who is the president and CEO of MOOG Automotive."

Then Luigi shared his business philosophy with me, and to this day, I have never forgotten it.

He said, "John, you are a bright young man with a good future in business. Please take my advice."

Luigi continued, "First, always treat your employees as if they are family. Second, spend the company's money as if it were your own. Third, never make any long-term financial commitment until you check with the board of directors."

To this day, I have never forgotten these words of wisdom. I seek each day to live by them. By the way, I was hired and spent nine rewarding years at MOOG Automotive.

Gianluigi Gabetti left a legacy of leadership by passing it on to me. You have that same opportunity to *pay it forward* every day as you relate to your employees.

The Legacy of Legacy

The legacy of leadership entails:

- Live the legacy today.
- Seek knowledge and leverage opportunities for others to grow, thereby creating a legacy for tomorrow.
- Each day create, teach, influence and advocate for others.
- Proactively influence others through trust, collaboration and open dialogue.
- Live your values.

- Inspire in word and in deed.
- Value differences in people and use them to create a learning organization.
- View employees as having unique and compelling contributions to make to the company.
- Building on the foundation of accountability and responsibility.
- Live and breathe leadership.

The legacy of successful leaders is to lead and provide a living legacy. Lead each day and leave a path for others to follow. That is the essence of high-touch leadership in a high-tech world.

Conclusion

The Magic of Touch

As I began the journey of writing this book, it caused me to relive many memorable and meaningful moments in my business career. Many of these moments carried over to my personal life. I always brought my job home with me, which took a toll on both my family and health at times. On the positive side, I was blessed to bring incredible *highs* to my home front as a result of the people that touched me.

Perhaps to the naked eye the concept of touch and leadership appear to be foreign and incompatible concepts.

My definition of *leadership touch* starts with hiring, training, developing, coaching and rewarding employees. It clearly recognizes the human side of the business enterprise, which means to appreciate and nurture the individuals you touch daily. This is communicated in your words, actions, behavior and facial expressions.

How does one put a value on a well-deserved pat on the back or things like remembering an employee's birthday? It sounds pretty elementary, but why do most managers not practice and appreciate *good people skills*? This is the clear and present danger of taking people for granted.

I suspect managers are busy meeting deadlines, preparing budgets and so forth. These are important activities and honorable endeavors. The danger is that by not properly engaging employees, morale is negatively impacted, creativity is stifled and open communication is thwarted.

Collaboration and true consensus building are sought and prized by today's employees—that is the magic of the human touch.

The human touch assists leaders in better understanding the human condition. As a result, they lift people up and truly hear their voice.

As the saying goes, "you can't take it with you." However, the human touch is what we will all eventually leave behind. The people we touch bank the positive memories and hopefully pass them on to the next generation.

The human touch is the compass and the North Star that guides employees to find their own song and voice.

> Collaboration and true consensus building are sought and prized by today's employees

In Italian, *Passante* means heavy on passing through. In essence, the honorable duty of being a leader with a *human touch* is a heavy assignment that requires strength of character, conviction, integrity, stamina, vision and clear focus. A very heavy job description.

In the truest sense, we are all passing through.

We must all choose to embrace technology. It is a powerful tool that helps us function better at our jobs. But at this juncture in the history of mankind, technology cannot emote concern, compassion, encouragement, feelings and a sense of true well-being. Only human beings with a heart and soul can do this.

You must never forget: There is no substitute for the wonderful magic of the human touch. A smile and a twinkle in the eye are an extension of the human touch. A smile can make a person's day and a twinkle in the eye can bring joy to others. It is okay to be human at work because people are the heart and soul of every organization.

We are judged by what we leave as our legacy.

The human touch leader is not soft. He or she sets high standards, drives performance, establishes clear expectations and holds others accountable. The human touch leader makes difficult decisions, rewards achievers, counsels the non-performers and if necessary terminates employees, but always in a humane and professional way.

The human side of the enterprise is the most difficult side because it affects the lives of others.

The Team

The Human Side:
High-Touch Leadership in a High-Tech World

Editor:
Gary McCoy, Fairway Communications

Copy Editor:
Deborah Render, Deborah S. Render Communications

Cover and Interior Design:
Lisa Haskin

Photography:
Mark Baltzley, Mark Baltzley Photography

Printing and Binding:
Yorke Printe Shoppe

The Organizational Development Group, Inc.

Founded by John A. Passante in 2003, The Organizational Development Group can help your organization increase its effectiveness by better utilizing your human capital.

The Organizational Development Group works within your organization to implement change initiatives, including:

- Management Development
- Leadership Development
- Personal Development
- Team Development
- Human Resource Programs and Policies
- Talent Assessment
- Strategic People Planning

Our goal is to increase the overall level of trust within your organization and among your employees.

The objective of The Organizational Development Group is to help its clients improve the ability and capacity to maximize both internal and external relationships, business challenges, organizational changes and growth initiatives.

John A. Passante and his staff provide professional executive and management recruiting services (search), executive coaching, leadership training seminars, and outplacement services. We also help support your M&A (mergers and acquisitions) activities. In addition, we conduct salary surveys, provide executive compensation reviews, implement performance recognition programs, and complete confidential assignments for CEO's and presidents.

Our goal is to drive peak performance by focusing on the human talent within your organization.

Contact Us
John A. Passante
President and CEO
The Organizational
Development Group, Inc.
46 Alfred Drowne Rd
Barrington, RI 02806-1806

401-252-9430

theorgdevgroup@gmail.com

About

John A. Passante

John A. Passante is a broad-based senior executive with over 35 years of extensive general marketing and sales, manufacturing, organizational development and senior human resource experience with progressive corporations involved in multiple locations, both domestic and international. He is the president and CEO of Brenton Productions, as well as the president and CEO of the Organizational Development Group, Inc. The firm specializes in recruiting, coaching, change management and culture enhancement. His clients include KYB America, Delphi, Wells Manufacturing, CATCO and AP Exhaust.

Passante has worked with corporations such as CARQUEST where he was senior vice president. He was also senior vice president, human resources for MOOG Automotive and senior director, worldwide human resources, sales and marketing for Delphi Products and Service Solutions. He has played a key strategic role in the integration of major global companies.

In 1995, Passante was inducted into the Automotive Aftermarket Hall of Fame and in August 1980, he received the University of Toledo Pacemaker Award, an award given annually to outstanding business alumni. In 1990, he received the Automotive Aftermarket Management Education Award from Northwood University.

Passante has earned the Automotive Aftermarket Professional (AAP) designation from the University of the Aftermarket. The AAP is awarded to those in the motor vehicle aftermarket who have demonstrated a dedication to the industry through ongoing professional development.

He is an adjunct professor at Northwood University and the University of the Aftermarket. He was also as a member of the Northwood University Board of Governors.

Brenton Productions became a Lifetime Trustee of University of the Aftermarket Foundation in 2013. As a result, Passante was appointed as a member of the University of the Aftermarket Foundation board of trustees.

Passante has been an adjunct professor at the University of Toledo, St. Louis University and a guest lecturer at Bowling Green State University, University of Missouri and Providence College. He is a member of the steering committee for the Global Automotive Aftermarket Symposium (GAAS) and for the GAAS Scholarship committee that annual grants scholarships to students studying for careers in the automotive aftermarket.

Passante is a motivational speaker who conducts many seminars for major corporations throughout the U.S., Canada and internationally. He has functioned as an internal consultant, facilitator and executive coach and is now bringing these multi-faceted management experiences and skills to the leadership of Brenton Productions, Inc. He has published many articles on leadership, communications and motivation and is the author of *The Human Side: High-Touch Leadership in a High-Tech World.*